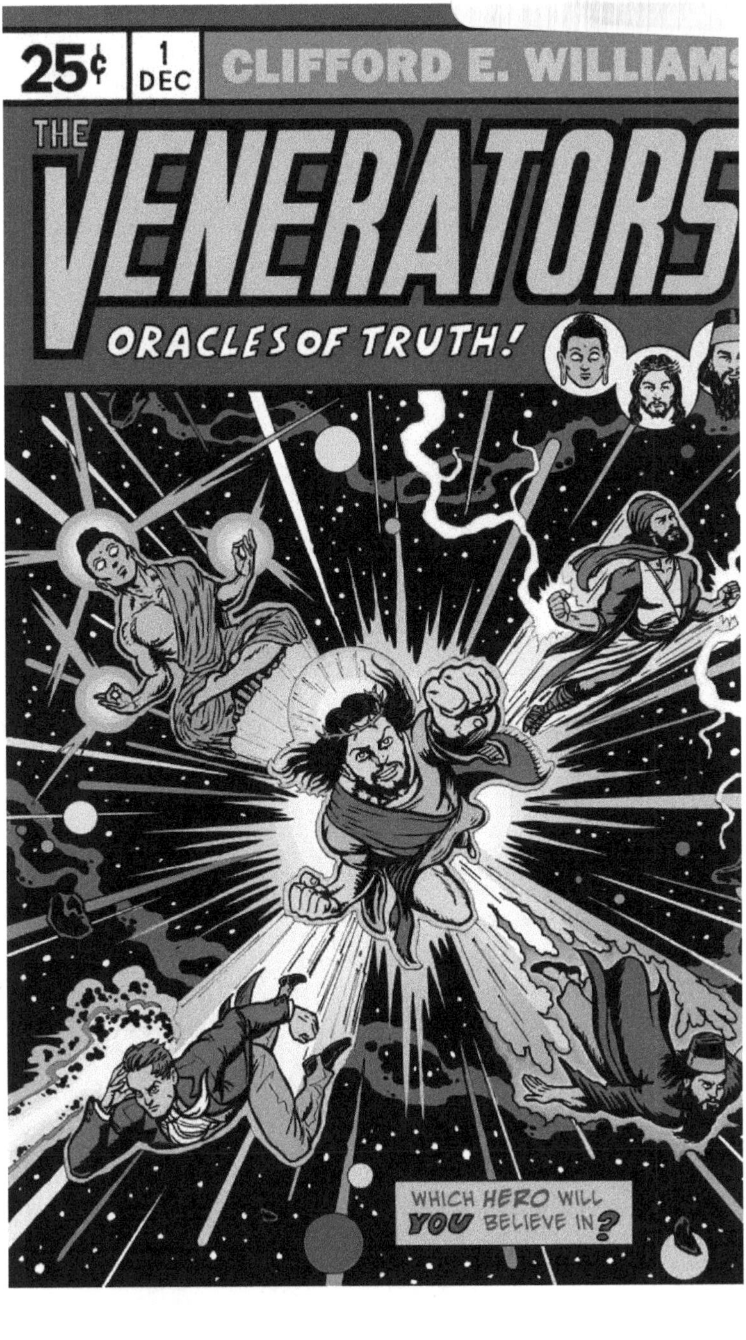

THE

Oracles of Truth

Clifford E. Williams

Acknowledgements

I have been thinking about this subject for over twenty years, and am excited to put my thoughts down in writing at last. However, we all build on the work of others so I have many to acknowledge. No one stands alone.

I would like to thank Josh McDowell, Norman Geisler, The Christian Research Institute, The Navigators, and The Institution for Creation Research for advancing my worldview and process of discovery. Please check them out on the web.

Additionally, prominent philosopher and mathematician Bertrand Russell deserves credit as the special atheist in my life. His book *Why I am Not a Christian* is more an emotional rather than a rational dissertation on Christianity, although I had high expectations of Mr. Russell, given his background in mathematics and rational thought. I was sure that if any untruths of Christianity existed, he would be the one to expose them. However, he was unable. In fact, he gave me the final push in my pursuit to find truth in Christianity, although I am sure he desired the opposite effect.

I also give credit to my mentors, especially Mike Kelf, who helped to encourage and guide me in my early faith.

I also thank Saul Haber for the amazing art work on the cover and inserts, http://comicbookman.com/. Great job!

"Then you will know the truth, and the truth will set you free."

—Jesus

"When I despair, I remember that all through history the way of truth and love have always won. There have been tyrants and murderers, and for a time, they can seem invincible, but in the end, they always fall. Think of it—always."

—Mahatma Gandhi

"Men occasionally stumble over the truth, but most of them pick themselves up and hurry off as if nothing ever happened."

—Winston Churchill

"In a time of deceit, telling the truth is a revolutionary act."

—George Orwell

Table of Contents

Acknowledgements 5

Preface 11

Introduction 18

We All Die 33

Something Happens 45

No One Knows 63

Many Speak 69

Stuck Trusting Someone 73

Jesus in Religion 90

Worst-Case Analysis 107

The Odds 127

The Deaths of Great Men 131

What Did They Say? 133

Why Some Do Not Trust 137

Conclusion 141

The Message 149

Your Choice 157

Appendix: Argument Simplified 161

About the Author 165

More Books by Clifford E. Williams..............................167

Preface

I am a follower of Jesus Christ. Since my late twenties, I have devoted my life to the way of Jesus. It is a life of sacrificial love for my family, friends, acquaintances, strangers, and enemies. I perform this devotion imperfectly, but I do not lack conviction or zeal. I would not live as such without Jesus's revelation, power, and guidance. This is His way—not my own. I am just trying to follow His example.

I am writing this as a friend to a friend, in the hope that I will encourage you to think about what is important. This subject deserves much thought and great care, because life is short and eternity is long. This book is not written to convince, but to inform. Of course, I have drawn strong conclusions in this area. But out of respect for you and your process, I will leave the strength of my conviction out of the picture. Instead, we will embark on a voyage of discovery. The information provided might help you to discover whom you can trust on the great questions of life: What is life about? and Where do we go when we die?

Or, as the band Radiohead has put it, "What the Hell am I doing here?"

What is more important than these questions? If I know the answer to the first, I will likely focus my life energy appropriately—which may affect how the answer to the second question impacts me.

Few people take time for this subject because it can seem overwhelming. There are thousands of volumes on the subject, most of which are based on speculation. There are many people who say they know the answers, and all the voices, similarities, and differences of those claiming to understand these great questions can create a world of confusion. Most of us quit before we have even started, feeling that there is no way to know truth in this matter. It is difficult to know whom we can trust.

So how would you discover whom to trust: by your preference, by your experience, or by random choice or luck?

Most of us hope there is a God. We are expecting to go to Heaven and hoping to never see Hell. If we have not lived up to God's expectations, we are relying on Him to let us slide, to overlook our iniquities. Anticipating Heaven, we look forward to seeing friends and family again, and secretly hope that the "jerks" of our past will not be there.

It is fair to say that we are all betting our souls on being right. We all know that hoping away Hell is a flimsy proposition, because there is no indication that such a hope will suffice to keep us safe after death. Nevertheless, how do we choose who will guide us to safety? Can we increase our odds, rather than gambling our souls in the hope of a lucky choice?

Religion is not scientific, nor is it mere faith. Lawyers, investigators, and scientists use tools of analysis to derive a road map to find truth, and so must we. Our beliefs are a decision we must make based on facts and probability. Given the facts, what religion is most likely to be true? Faith follows!

According to Occam's Razor, the scenario that is most likely to be true is the one that makes the fewest assumptions. For example, if I cannot find my keys it would be less likely that ninjas took my keys and more likely that I misplaced them. A strange and improbable set of events would have to occur in order for me to conclude that ninjas have my keys.

Occam's Razor can be used to determine the existence of God.

For example, the nature of our universe has lead us to observe that every cause has an effect. This means that something does not come from nothing, so there must an initial cause that created everything. Even if you believe in the Big Bang, or that we exist because of evolution or aliens, one must ask, "What or who started it all?"

This is God! He is the Great uncaused cause.

In the beginning, there was God.

Chaos could not form the ordered universe we live in. To explain that the Universe developed by chance would require too many assumptions. According to Occam's razor, the wild set of assumptions needed to create a universe by chance makes chance an implausible explanation. You would assume everything has beginning but the universe. You would assume that the universe is mindless without laws and the laws of the universe just happened, that energy comes from nothing, that rocks turn into living mindful, willfull humans by chance which is a short list of wild assumptions.

It is in fact most plausible that God created the Universe and established physical laws for it to operate by. There is only one assumption based on observable fact! There is a creation and the assumption is it needs a Creator: That's God!

I mention all this to emphasize that it is necessary to use analysis when considering what or whom to believe. We rarely make decisions based on a knowledge of absolute truth—there is too little that can be absolutely known. Rather, we make decisions based on whom we trust and what we hope. We make decisions on marriage, family, and careers based on the information available to us at the time. We decide to trust the people on whom we depend and hope that our choices will work out for the best. Sometimes they work out, and other times they do not.

Nevertheless, I think we need to do more to prepare for the next life, more than just hope for something good. Engineers and scientists use knowledge, data, and facts in order to prepare for the unknown. For example, space shuttles and bridges are not built to minimum standards. This is because, even though engineers know a lot, they also know that they do not know everything. Earthquakes, tornadoes, imperfections in construction materials, and other factors are out of the engineer's control, so they overbuild in order to ensure integrity of structure. They plan for the what-ifs and prepare for the just-in-case scenarios. After all, the possibility that a bridge might fall or that a shuttle might not bring its occupants home safely demand a "hope for the best and prepare for the worst" philosophy.

When I was learning to rock climb, my mentor told me, "We protect not for the likelihood of a fall but for the consequences!" And when it comes to your life, and death, so should you! There is much more at stake when we are considering the afterlife than a broken arm or a mangled spine.

The Tacoma Narrows Bridge in Washington State fell before I was born. At a mile long, it was the fifth largest suspension bridge in the world. In 1940, only four months after it opened, the bridge fell because a 42 mph wind blew it apart. Despite the engineer's expertise, the bridge fell. Sometimes, even with knowledge and preparation for the unexpected, things do not work out. You see? What you *do not know* can cause disaster.

In 1950, the Narrows Bridge was rebuilt with a new design, and another bridge was added by its side in 2007. Both stand strong! Because we have learned from the mistakes of the past, we can build a better future.

While an engineer can learn how to build a better, safer bridge, when it comes to death and the afterlife, we might only get one chance to get it right. Consequently, we must use the approach of a good engineer; when in doubt, take extra precautions and overbuild. After all, our souls are at stake.

Introduction

> "Life is hard. Then you die. Then they throw dirt
> in your face. Then the worms eat you.
> Be grateful it happens in that order."
>
> —David Gerrold

We joke about death because we do not know what else to do about it. It is out of our hands. We stay busy in order to avoid the great questions of life. We spend a lot of time trying to find peace, relaxation, and fun. Thus, it is no great surprise that the word "diversion" can be used to mean either "hobby" or "purposeful distraction technique." We engage in diversions on purpose to entertain our time and money. Sadly, these have been our response to the pressure of considering the meaning of life. We stay busy in order to avoid thinking about these important issues.

Before I began to follow Jesus, I remember saying, "If there is a God, I'm sure he put me here to have a good time. And I won't disappoint him!" It was a stupid thing to say. My philosophy was that I should make a lot of money and spend it to enjoy myself. I aimed to live through my diversions, thus avoiding thoughts of the inevitability of death. At this time, I practiced what I now call "Meism." Meism is our "personal" religion, one that insists that life "is all about me!"

The pursuit of enjoyment seemed the rational way to live my life. What else would I do? Why not enjoy myself? As part of this, I decided that I needed a wife, a high paying and personally esteeming profession, and to enjoy the fruits of my labor. Kids were an accepted part of all this, one that my wife required for a good life. Of course, I could see the joy in having a family, and I knew the cost as well.

I treated people as nicely as I needed to in order to enjoy life. Some people fit into my life, and others did not. Some friends were fun, some had money, but some were a pain, and better to be avoided. When it came to people who impeded my pursuit of enjoyment, I simply put up with them.

We live in a postmodern age. We cannot escape it; it is our matrix for understanding the world. Socially, we have concluded that institutions cannot be trusted, and that includes religion! Banks, businesses, religious organizations, and governments have all failed us. They have shown themselves to be full of lies and contradictions. These organizations are just systematic groups of Meists, who organize to gain more for themselves.

Nevertheless, before we get too uppity, we should confess that we are Meists also. We can hardly help focusing on what is best for ourselves—it is an instinct, after all. But we can acknowledge that it is not the best part of ourselves, and we can try not to be hypocritical Meists.

Even philanthropy and niceness are suspect. We know the Meist only does well for selfish reasons. For the wealthy Meist, acting charitably soothes the conscience of knowing that others are in need. Middle class Meists give to feel good. Five bucks given to the sign-waver on the corner does wonders for the Meist's smile.

Additionally, religious Meists are suspect. They receive enjoyment from their religion because it makes them feel morally elevated. They are kind and charitable in order to go to Heaven, which is certainly a selfish pursuit.

Many seekers of truth have given up because of all the hypocrisy they see in others and in themselves.

And really, what is truth? We read history and the news and conclude that everyone has his own truth. Each religion is pointing in a different direction. We sense that we could never know the truth, so we opt out of the exploration. Like sheep we stay with the flock; even as it tumbles over the cliff, we bleat, "There is no truth! There is no truth!"

We determine that if truth cannot be found, we will make our own. The individual religion of the Meist is formed through this reasoning. Everyone chooses his own truth to support his personal desires.

We suspect that much of our worldview is formed by others and not derived by our own experience. We see that the precepts we grew up with were forced on us, not formed through free thinking. Our parents and culture gave us our worldview and, because of this, we do not trust in the truth of what we have been given. We know that if we were born in Saudi Arabia, we would be Muslims and if we were born in the Soviet Union in the 1970s, we would be atheists.

We are in a vertigo, dizzied by all the information available to us: there is a God and there is not a God. God is thus or not thus, and therefore the reason for living is this or that. Because of this lack of substantial clarity in the nature of God, we give up on caring about larger issues and live for ourselves. (Which is not surprising, since it is what we desired in the first place.) We complain about the world and despondently anesthetize ourselves with diversions: drugs, alcohol, leisure, sports, entertainment, family, achievement, religion, and education.

A strange matrix is developed. Self-satisfaction becomes our guide and experience becomes our truth. If you had bad parents, then you may conclude that all families are just as bad. If Mom and Dad were good and went to church, then you may conclude, "A good person goes to church." If you tend to steal and lie, it is easy to conclude that the rest of the world is doing the same. Because of these differing experiences, we draw different conclusions on various important subjects. We meet others who have formed different conclusions—we know that everyone looks at the world a little differently and, as a result, we are reluctant to draw hard truths. How can anyone be certain of anything, when there is nothing that we can all agree on?

We distrust dogma, especially. Secular Humanists, Nazis, Democrats, and Muslims all have a worldview and call it the truth. Many of these views are dogmatic and even militant, but today it is hard to accept adamant opinions. Anyone who is so sure of life and death must be foolish, un-thoughtful, and ignorant to insist that the truth can be known when anyone can see that no one knows anything for sure.

Those who act sure about what they believe are generally basing their opinions on their lived experiences. They might say, "I prayed and God answered, so God is real" or "I prayed and nothing happened, so there is no God."

Therefore, each person draws up his or her allegiances according to his experiences, and then vows that he knows the truth. No one is exempt from this phenomenon. We must draw certain conclusions in order to navigate through life. Even if the foundation of your knowledge is, "Nothing is knowable," you have still drawn a conclusion about the nature of knowledge, and this provides a definitive perspective for your life. Thus, no one can stand in judgment over another, because we are all blind and balancing on the platform of the beliefs that we think we can live by.

Being tethered to a set of beliefs can give a sense of stability and purpose, but it doesn't work for everyone. Maybe that is why the suicide rates have increased in the past few years. Currently, suicide rates are the highest they have ever been in the U.S., at 12.4 suicides per 100,000 people. It has exceeded car crashes as the number one cause of death.[1] Kurt Cobain killed himself in the prime of life; it apparently made sense to him at the time. According to him, "It's better to burn out than fade away."

If life has no meaning, no real purpose, then why live poor and hopeless? Why live in pain for a holiday of happiness?

In today's society, the majority of people find their purpose in basing their lives on the pursuit of peace and pleasure. Many believe that religion is obsolete. They have traded the promise of Heaven for a grand life on earth. Nevertheless, these pleasure-seekers do have a sort of religion: a mix of pluralism, relativism, and skepticism. Pluralism holds, "All religions are significant and true in

---

[1] http://firstwatch.jwatch.org/cgi/content/full/2012/927/2

their own way." Relativism holds that culture and perspective determine whether an act is morally wrong. Skepticism locks the door of our purgatorial catacomb with the cry, "There is no truth!"

Welcome to the New Age, where there is no law, no God, no reason, no purpose, no destiny.

Today's society has concluded that, because there is no knowable truth about philosophy and religion, we should do our best to avoid hindrances and pain. As individuals, we have cast off the burden of truth because it is difficult, potentially unpleasant, and perceived as unknowable.

But you will never find answers when the first conclusion drawn is that there is no answer. You will never even begin to wonder. Perhaps the truth is unknowable, or perhaps we shy away from the truth because we fear that the immortal lines from *A Few Good Men* are right: "You can't handle the truth!"

We have become nihilists to varying degrees. You might think that a nihilist is nothing but a punk rocker, but the punk is just the skin on the nihilistic idea. I do not wear metallic-face art or a mohawk, but we all agree with these metal-studded outcasts to some degree. However, we frame these ideas in more refined language, using less extreme terms, because we are more moderate than the punk rocker. Still, it all comes down to one vital concept: life is without meaning. It merely exists for its own sake.

You may have given answers to these questions for your own life, and they might be more or less nihilist or religious in nature. Having these answers helps to temporarily soothe the distress.

I know that it is natural to want to have fun and avoid pain. This inclination drives us all, to some degree. Most of us do not throw off all restraint, but continue to fulfill the duties of life. We go to work, school, and funerals. We weigh our values and desires and make compromises to this end. We are trying to maximize our pleasure and minimize our pain.

Life is tough! Moreover, life is hard enough without troubling ourselves with challenging issues and tough questions. Who can know what happens when we die? If Einstein cannot answer it, how can we?

But really, it does not take Einstein's brilliance to determine what happens after death. Rather, it takes courage to ask these questions. After all, we might not like the answers. The answers may require us to make difficult changes in our lives.

And furthermore, what if you come close to an answer, but do not have absolute certainty in it? Whom can you trust to guide you? What happens if you do nothing?

Yes, it is difficult to find answers to these questions, but we must bravely address this subject.

I suppose it is self-evident that we get to make our own decisions for our lives. This is the gift of self-determination. I have the liberty to do with my life what I chose. Or, as Jimi Hendrix put it, "I'm the one that's got to die when it's time for me to die, so let me live my life the way I want to."

But have you ever thought about the risks and the potential associated with this gift? You have a great opportunity to live the most incredible life, and share this life for the benefit of others. You can also live to the lowest levels of depravity; you can be a cancer to your family, spreading it to the community and the world.

This book will go through a simple process of analysis to help you meditate on the great questions of life and the finality of death. Here is a framework of what we know, to help us look at the issue.

1. We all die.
2. Something happens.
3. No one knows for sure what happens.
4. We have to trust someone in order to understand what happens.
5. We must consider whom we trust, and why.

These are indisputable facts. We die and something happens. But what happens? Will it be good or bad? Will God warmly welcome us, or will there be pain and punishment?

No one knows for sure what happens. Some people who have medically died and then were revived claim that they saw a light. They said it was warm, welcoming, and peaceful. Even supposing that this experience is something we can all expect to have upon death, it does not answer the essential question. These people were "dead" for a short time, only. They did not truly dwell there on the other side.

Many have claimed to know what happens. Religions are formed around these claims. These religions answer the questions of why we live and what happens after we die. They each have their own take on the issue. There are similarities among them, but also critical differences.

Because of the plethora of options, we cannot know for certain which answer is the correct one. Thus, we are stuck trusting someone.

Whom do you trust?

I have asked atheists this question, and I was surprised at how many have said that they only trust themselves on this issue. I wonder what they know that I don't about the afterlife that gives them so much trust in themselves.

We start with the question. We start with the assumption that the answer is available. After all, if you conclude at the onset that there is no answer, then you will never seek an answer, let alone find one. If you have any doubt about the idea that the answer is unknowable, then it is safer to assume that there *is* an answer, and that it is knowable.

If there is a God, He may have expectations, after all. He may have qualifiers for the afterlife. And if so, we need

God to show us what to do. This is our only hope—our souls may be at stake. As Audioslave's Chris Cornel asserts, ". . . my Creator. You gave me life; now show me how to live."

Yeah, I like that insight: "show me how to live." This is very thoughtful. God created us and we need Him to show us the truth!

We All Die

"I'm not afraid of death;
I just don't want to be there when it happens."
—*Woody Allen*

Mr. Allen makes light of death while admitting the gravity of it. I also do not like the idea of death. I never thought about it much growing up, but I do recall thinking about it once, when I was very young. I could not imagine what it would be like to be dead, to not exist. I could only remember life—life was the only experience I'd had. The concept of death was like being told that the stars go on forever as I gazed upon the depths of the Universe. (Of course, now I have heard that the Universe does not extend to infinity, which leaves a still greater mystery: What is beyond the stars—infinite emptiness? Yeah, it still freaks me out.)

When I was young, I thought death was for the unlucky and the old. I was not old and I did not feel unlucky, so death was not something I needed to think about. All I needed to concern myself with was living.

I was full of goals and aspirations: for a career, for a family, for a life like everyone else's. I wanted to run marathons and triathlons, climb mountains and be financially secure. I wanted to enjoy my life.

I left high school in need of a career that would fund the cool life I aimed to have. I studied engineering because I'd heard there were jobs and good money.

I met a girl in college whom I went on to marry. We had our first and second children while I was still attending the University.

After college and a year of Air Force Training, I landed my first job—the job I had worked for in college. It offered good money, security, and prestige. My wife and I started dreaming how we would spend our money and get on living the good life.

This began the next phase of my life. Finally, I had achieved my goals.

But I was still not satisfied. I would drive to work thinking, "Is this it? Really? Get a job, have some good times, grow up the kids, retire, and die?" I wondered in horror: "This was my destiny?" My mind rejected the idea.

I decided to find another way to fulfill my life. I began thinking about graduate school. It was another goal. It would give my life a purpose. I re-applied to the Mathematics Department at Washington State University to work toward a PhD.

But still, as I drove to work each day, I had time to think. I would ask myself, "What happens when I earn my PhD? Will that be enough?" I began to realize that I was just chasing my tail—pursuing more just for the sake of pursuing something. Up until this point in my life, setting and achieving goals were all I had ever done. I had used goals as a distraction and pushed the larger questions of life down the road.

And I began to realize that my desire for more would never be satiated.

Now, for the first time, I thought about the meaning of life. Was it simply to live and die like a dog? I could not—I would not accept this answer. There had to be more to life than just living!

Thus began my pursuit of the truth.

I was never very polished, culturally speaking. I could be rough and sharp. If I wanted to cuss, I did. If you pissed me off, I would let you have it. I did not care what others thought of me, unless it might negatively affect me. I was very aggressive in sports and I only had time for what would advance me and my life (fortunately, this included my family).

I did not do drugs or drink to excess. I was good to my wife and kids, or at least as good as I was capable of at the time.

I hated church meetings and I had mixed feelings about being a Christian. I liked Jesus from a distance, but I did not fit in with the church community. Despite this, I decided to take my family to church. At a minimum, I thought, it would be good for my family.

I went to church and I hated it. People were praying loud and some were crying. Some were speaking in tongues. I felt very uncomfortable. I was experiencing culture shock! I thought the scenario was weird and ridiculous, but I pushed myself past the strange experience.

When I entered that chamber of perceived torture—the church—I did not want to talk to anyone. I looked down at my feet and quickly found a seat. I am sure I gave an aura of: "Do not screw with me!" I knew that I was "bad" compared to these good Christians, and the less they realized it, the better.

The service, on the other hand, was nice. I liked the message. It was interesting. I had not heard much in the way of theology before, and I was open to learn. Actually, I was desperate.

After a month of Sundays, I drug my feet to follow Jesus. This was due to my psychological and emotional need for answers. It had nothing to do with truth or having a spiritual experience.

I grew up in a Christian culture, so I guessed I was a Christian. I remember when I joined the Air Force, I filled out a form that asked if I was Catholic or Protestant. I answered Protestant, because I knew I was not a Catholic. (They put this designation on your dog tag, which doubled as a toe-tag if you died in combat. It told the Air Force which religious leader should attend to your funeral.)

While attending church regularly, I began to ask myself, "Why can't I be a Muslim or a Jew? What is right?"

I figured that it was possible to know what religion was true, and so I began my studies.

I studied for another reason, as well. I knew that, if I were to be a Christian, I would have to be able to defend my position. I worked with many engineers who had degrees in physics, engineering, and other sciences. I was too proud to believe something that was indefensible. I could not imagine anyone following a belief system that was not based in truth, that was not backed up by solid evidence. If something was not justifiable, why would you follow it?

I studied and discovered who I have put my money on: Jesus.

Death is inescapable. This fact creates only three options for understanding death: 1) ignore the fact that you know nothing about it; 2) find a religion that suits you; or 3) discover the truth. I did not want religion—I wanted to know the truth. Ignorance was not an option; for me, denial of death could not soothe the pain of life. Nor could I choose just any religion to stop the bleeding. I wanted real answers—answers that healed.

Death is real and there is no reason to believe it is not permanent. Dig up a grave and you will find the remnants of a life lived. It does not matter if the people were good or bad, rich or poor: they are all bones, now.

Death is the scariest subject in the world to contemplate. It is so important—it happens to all of us—and yet it is entirely unknowable, for no one who's experienced it can share what it is like. We all tend to draw conclusions to make the issue go away. I have heard some incredibly irrational conclusions drawn on this subject, as a result. I have sorted the people who create these conclusions into six categories: Sensationalists, Daredevils, Goodies, Hardcores, Procrastinators, and Nothings.

The Sensationalists have experienced goose bumps at their particular religious service. Endorphins flowed, a burning arose in their bosoms, or they felt that they were slain in the spirit. For the Sensationalists, this feeling confirms their religious views. Because they were in the woods appreciating God's bounty or in a religious service when the moment occurred, they conclude, "It was God!" Moreover, they conclude that this experience was not only a confirmation of God's existence, but also a confirmation of His personal approval and acceptance. Thus, for Sensationalists, the case is closed. This would be considered crumby detective work!

Daredevils are those who say, "I don't care if I go to Hell!" They live their way and will not be hindered. When I was an engineer, I had a friend with a PhD in Astrophysics with whom I would discuss religion. I would give him books that explained why he should trust Jesus. He politely told me, one day, "Cliff, if there is a God, I still do not want to serve Him." I respected his poorly thought-out opinion, for at least he was honest. He obviously had slipped himself a mickey. What about death and the afterlife? Those who say they do not care about Hell are responding emotionally to avoid the discussion. They squint their eyes, plug their ears, and sing loud in order to keep from knowing the answer. After all, knowing it may cramp their style. They are willing to risk everything on the hope that the spiritual realm does not exist.

When the truth is, if Hell existed and they were there, they would want out.

In order to make them think, I have said, "Dude, I can prove you would care if you went to Hell. If I simply twisted your nose with a pair of pliers, you would beg to have me stop and you would do anything in your power to relieve the pain."

If you say you don't care if you go to Hell, you are ignoring what Hell is!

Goodies say, "I believe that God is good and will take me to Heaven because He knows my heart." Unfortunately, there are a great many unfounded assumptions built into this statement. It is like going to a stranger's house, inviting yourself in, and expecting to live there without expectations of payment or responsibility. It is like saying, "I'm such a nice person, who wouldn't want me to bless their home by my presence?" It sounds silly to put it this way, but the silliness accentuates the absurdity of the Goodies' laissez-faire conclusion.

The Hardcores are interesting. They are the religious zealots. They believe something is true because they believe it is true, and their faith is their only foundation. Hardcores make good suicide bombers. They do not listen to others or learn from their mistakes. Anything that is counter to their belief is automatically rejected without thought or reason. They are dogmatic and at times overbearing. It is usually a challenge to spend time around Hardcores.

Procrastinators have a certain system of belief, but know they are not living to that standard. They say, "I will do it later." I know a handful of people who are living this way, many of them young people. They want to play and enjoy life for now, and decide that they will follow God's instructions when they are "old." Some are comfortable waiting to make things right with God on their death beds. I find this lifestyle disgusting and ridiculous, and do not have much respect for procrastinators. They remind me of a spouse who says, "I love you, Baby!", and then sleeps around. They want the benefits of Heaven without the responsibilities on earth.

The Nothings are those who like the idea of living and dying like a dog, with no care for their souls or the afterlife. They ignore death and say, "Nothing happens when you die." This can be very freeing for a time, as it allows maximum freedom. Nothings can do what they want and live for themselves. Regardless of what you might expect,

Nothings are not necessarily complete hedonists; they may exercise the golden rule and avoid the extremes in their free living. Of course, some gorge themselves on life.

The reality of death forces us to make conclusions about what it means for us. We seek a psychological refuge. Is this a weakness or is it reasonable? Is it only natural for us to accept these conclusions without proof? I believe we should be curious about death, and should not be afraid to ask the hard questions in order to understand it better. I believe that these realities should drive us to the question, "What happens when we die?" Thinking is good, but not if we use it simply to grab at ideas that sedate our fears. To do so justifies Carl Marx's disparaging opinion that religion is "the opiate of the masses." (Nevertheless, Marx sedated his fear, though not with religion; he looked down on religious types while he lay in his own psychological drug den.)

I like what Da Vinci said, and I think he was right!

"While I thought that I was learning how to live, I have been learning how to die."

Something Happens

> "For death is no more than a turning of us over from time to eternity."
>
> —William Penn

It is irrefutable that something happens when you die. At minimum, there is a change of state from consciousness to unconsciousness. The question is, what happens after you die? There are several possibilities, including Nirvana, Reincarnation, Heaven, Hell, and nothing. Which do you prefer?

I wish that my preference formed reality. Life would be really cool. I would make it so I could never lose. I would prefer to still have my twenty-five-year-old body. I would prefer to be smarter, have more money, and be more persuasive. We would all prefer to change certain things. But, in spite of our wishes, we have limitations due to gender, race, nationality, socio-economics, where you were born, parents, spouses, children, health, intellect, and desire, which all influence our reality. These help to create our current state, and most are out of our control. Wishful thinking won't change them. We can only maximize our reality by actively trying to improve it.

Reality will determine what happens, not imagination. We can sedate ourselves during our lifetimes with a certain set of desire-driven beliefs, but the moment we enter the afterlife, all will be known, despite our former life's preferences. This much is clear—preferences do not create reality.

The state of our souls after death may be an ascension to Nirvana, but it could also be reincarnation, Heaven, Hell, or nothing. Deaths is imminent, followed by an uncertain outcome.

Reincarnation

"[One] time he was asked if he believed in an afterlife. After a moment's hesitation he said no, that he thought there was only 'some kind of velvety cool blackness,' adding then: 'Of course, I admit I may be wrong. It is conceivable that I might well be reborn as a Chinese coolie. In such case I should lodge a protest.'"

—Sir Winston Churchill

We have all heard of reincarnation. I think a lot people have chosen to believe that this is what happens after death. Ideas such as reincarnation have no real impact on your life, which makes them fun to toy with. Most people who believe in reincarnation believe that, if you are good enough, you will evolve spiritually to a higher state of being after you die and are reborn. Of course, if you are bad, you could become a dung beetle or worse.
According to Wikipedia:

> Reincarnation is the religious or philosophical concept that the soul or spirit, after biological death, begins a new life in a new body that may be human, animal or spiritual depending on the moral quality of the previous life's actions. This doctrine is a central tenet of the Indian religions and is a belief that was held by such historic figures as Pythagoras, Plato and Socrates. It is also a common belief of pagan religions such as Druidism, Spiritism, Theosophy, and Eckankar and is found in many tribal societies around the

world, in places such as Siberia, West Africa, North America, and Australia.[2]

In fact, the Foo Fighters have a song that contemplates the concept of reincarnation:

"End Over End"

Burn all the candles out.
Make a wish, but not aloud.
Re-live the here and now
To see you now and then.
I'm a revolving door.
I've seen it all before.
I will begin again,
But I can't start until I've seen the end.[3]

I like how many modern music artists explore the world and life through song. In, "End over End," the writer delves into the concept of reincarnation. It is a fun musing. What if we are reborn? What if we meet again: me as a

---

[2] http://en.wikipedia.org/wiki/Reincarnation
[3] http://www.azlyrics.com/lyrics/foofighters/endoverend.html

worm and you as a bird? Will you eat me or recognize me as a friend? It is an interesting concept to ponder, at the least.

Nirvana

> "I have been born more times than anybody except Krishna."
>
> —Mark Twain

The ideas of Nirvana and Reincarnation were primarily derived from Hinduism. Siddhartha Gautama, the first Buddha, or "Enlightened One," adapted Hindu philosophies and thereby founded Buddhism. Nirvana is present in both philosophies.

According to Wikipedia, Nirvana is:

> An ancient Sanskrit term used in Indian religions to describe the profound peace of mind that is acquired with moksha (liberation). In shramanic thought, it is the state of being free from suffering. In Hindu philosophy, it is union with the Brahman (Supreme Being).

The word literally means "blown out" (as in a candle) and refers, in the Buddhist context, to the imperturbable stillness of mind after the fires of desire, aversion, and delusion have been finally extinguished.[4]

Since Buddhism is derived from Hinduism, it is not surprising that they both have a concept of Nirvana. As described above, Nirvana is a state without suffering, under which one is united spiritually with the god-figure Brahman. It sounds a lot like the Heaven of the Koran and the Bible, but it is different in several essential ways.

You gain Nirvana by being "good," although it is not exactly clear what "good" is. Your Karma determines your destiny, whether you are born in your next life either lower or higher on the spiritual evolutionary ladder to Nirvana.

With Buddhism, Nirvana is achieved by following the prescription of the Four Fold Truths, by which one can attain this state of non-conscious spiritual existence united with a non-material, non-personal Brahma. This concept of Nirvana is different from the Hindu concept, which holds that Nirvana is a conscious eternal existence.

One website describes Nirvana thus:

---

[4] http://en.wikipedia.org/wiki/Nirvana

> I am sick of this cycle of reincarnation. I don't want to reincarnate anymore on earth. This is a prison planet. I don't know if this feeling stems from that fact that we are closer to 2012 or if this is just my male testosterone issues.
>
> 1. Does anyone else feel this way about reincarnating on this prison planet?
> 2. How do we end this cycle?
> 3. Why do we choose to reincarnate here? And do we have a choice?[5]

It is interesting to read the responses to this query, which help us understand the dilemmas of reincarnation. These include:

- "get off the wheel of karma... how? Forgive and let go."
- "Well, don't go to the light for one. :)"
- "amen..."
- "yes don't go to the light. trust [me,] i was in a coma that's what got me back to this place there must be some way out of here."[6]

---

[5] http://www.godlikeproductions.com/forum1/message943145/pg1
[6] http://www.godlikeproductions.com/forum1/message943145/pg1

It is unclear. You can see these people are having trouble. The concept is a little slippery.

It is possible that, after you die, you could reach the place of perfection if you are qualified. But if not, you will be reincarnated, either up or down the ladder of the soul's evolution.

Annihilation

Annihilation is non-existence. Many believe that, after death, you no longer exist materially or spiritually. This idea is held by atheists, Jehovah's Witnesses, and a small sect of Christians. The Buddhist belief is a modification of annihilation, as they describe Nirvana as existing after death without consciousness. There is not much of a difference between existing and not existing, after all, if you are not aware of the fact.

I dig the idea of annihilation. If I could choose truth, it has my vote. According to Wikipedia:

> Annihilationism (from Latin annihilō) is a
> Christian belief that apart from salvation the

death of human beings results in their total destruction (annihilation) rather than their everlasting torment. It is directly related to the doctrine of conditional immortality, the idea that a human soul is not immortal unless it is given eternal life.[7]

They call this a Christian view, but the idea of annihilation is not the historical or traditional view expressed in Christian theology. Some individual Christians and the Jehovah's Witnesses adhere to this idea, however.

It is worthwhile to look to the words of proponents of this idea, who are primarily atheists:

> I cannot conceive of a God who rewards and punishes his creatures, or has a will of the kind that we experience in ourselves. Neither can I nor would I want to conceive of an individual that survives his physical death; let feeble souls, from fear or absurd egoism, cherish such thoughts. I

[7] http://en.wikipedia.org/wiki/Annihilationism

am satisfied with the mystery of the eternity of life and with the awareness and a glimpse of the marvelous structure of the existing world, together with the devoted striving to comprehend a portion, be it ever so tiny, of the Reason that manifests itself in nature.[8]

I'm an atheist, and I don't have any belief in an afterlife. You could say that I'm resigned to the fact that this wonderful life that we get here is it. And having hit 60, it's a good time to get resigned to these things and not be too nervous or upset— and enjoy what great times one can have.[9]
Faith means not wanting to know what is true.[10]

I have never seen the slightest scientific proof of the religious ideas of heaven and hell, of future life for

---

[8] Albert Einstein, The World As I See It
http://atheism.about.com/od/einsteingodreligion/tp/Einstein-Quotes-on-Afterlife.htm
[9] David Gilmour
http://www.quotesdaddy.com/quote/239286/David+Gilmour/im-an-atheist-and-i-dont-have-any-belief-in-an-afterlife
[10] Friedrich Nietzsche http://thinkexist.com/quotation/-faith-means_not_wanting_to_know_what_is/175794.html

individuals, or of a personal God. So far as religion of the day is concerned, it is a damned fake . . . . Religion is all bunk.[11]

I guess we can deduce from these intelligent men that only stupid people believe in God and the afterlife. They pit their intelligence, avarice, and hopelessness against trust and hope. They trust nothing but their own observation. The obvious danger in this is that they may be wrong; the potential consequences of being wrong on this point are too severe to be flippant. Which is why the following quote from Stekel always gives me a chuckle: "Fervid atheism is usually a screen for repressed religion."[12]

There may be an answer to the question that these atheists have no answer for. It takes courage to try. Everyone moves through life and is allowed to draw his own conclusions. Still, this freedom makes for a risky game, when it comes to the afterlife.

---

[11] Thomas Edison http://quotationsbook.com/quote/45814/
[12] Wilhelm Stekel http://www.notable-quotes.com/a/atheism_quotes.html

Heaven

> "In heaven, all the interesting people are missing."
> —Friedrich Nietzsche[13]

If there is a Heaven, then it makes sense that everyone would want to go. Heaven is "The abode of God, the angels, and the spirits of the righteous after death; the place or state of existence of the blessed after the mortal life."[14] It is a place of love and freedom, and lacks the pain we currently endure. There is no war, no hunger or rape, no violence, no torment, and no injustice. Prejudice ceases and hate evaporates. In heaven, all our questions are answered. We will be with our loved ones. It seems pretty inviting, doesn't it? However, I have read quotes from many "smart" people who say that they wouldn't want to go to heaven.

It is enough to say that, if there is a Heaven, everyone wants to go there. The tricky part is, whom

---

[13] http://www.goodreads.com/quotes/tag?utf8=%E2%9C%93&id=heaven
[14] http://dictionary.reference.com/browse/heaven

should we trust to guide us on a path to heaven? Choosing well may make the difference because, according to some religions, not all paths lead to heaven.

Furthermore, you must do more than simply choose one religious leader over another—you must submit to the ideas this leader promotes in order to reach heaven. It is not enough to put a check in the right box—you must adhere to the way. This is what it means to be part of a certain religion—observing the practices that the group has determined will honor your god.

I once met a young lady who said she was a Jew. She was not Jewish by bloodline, but by choice. I asked, "What is it like keeping the 613 laws of the Torah? How does it work?" Her face deformed and she replied with a foul remark before walking off. I did not mean to put her off, but I did not really think she was truly practicing Judaism, given that she was from a small town in the Northwest.

What we decide may radically change our lives; if we choose well, a better place may be in store for us.

Hell

"I hold it to be the inalienable right of anybody to go to hell in his own way."

—Robert Frost[15]

Robert Frost is right—there is more than one way to Hell, and we have a lot of freedom to choose our path.

I think Hell is well-understood by most. All major religions contain a concept of Hell, although there are variations in the duration and types of punishment, and the behaviors that will bring you there. In all, however, it is a place of torment for those who qualify. According to the strict definition, Hell is "The place or state of punishment of the wicked after death; the abode of evil and condemned spirits; Gehenna or Tartarus."[16]   Hell is a great motivator toward religion. After all, who would want to go there, if it exists? Hell seems like such a terrible place you would want to do whatever it takes to go anywhere else.

---

[15] http://www.goodreads.com/quotes/tag?utf8=%E2%9C%93&id=hell
[16] http://dictionary.reference.com/browse/hell?s=t

It also makes sense that the most evil people really should not be allowed into Heaven. The most vile and wicked should be punished for their atrocities committed on Earth. I'm talking about guys such as Moa and Stalin, who were guilty of killing 70 million people. If there is a Hell, I will bet those two are there.

There are those who believe that God would not make Hell, that it is too horrible a place for a loving God to create. Especially the Christian view, which holds that Hell lasts for eternity. After all, shouldn't the punishment fit the crime?

Hey, I get where you're coming from! If I were in charge, maybe I would not create Hell. Maybe I would just make bad people vanish instantly on the spot if they committed certain violations of what I thought was good. Actually, if the universe operated that way, I may have been erased by now, due to my own decry.

It is interesting to note that people who believe in Hell commit fewer crimes than those who believe that there is only a Heaven.[17] That goes to reason. If you do not believe

---

[17] http://seattle.cbslocal.com/2012/06/22/study-finds-people-who-believe-in-heaven-commit-more-crimes/

in Hell, then at least you can comfort yourself that there will be no eternal consequences for your actions on earth. Of course, there may be a temporal price to pay, but these are just temporary. However, if you believe that God will punish evil in the afterlife, you might think twice before committing your next felony.

This mentality could account for the high incarceration rate in the United States. Since 1980, the incarceration rate went from about 500,000 to nearly 2.5 million. It has increased nearly 400% in thirty years.[18] It makes you think! Hell may or may not be real, but it still affects our actions on earth.[19]

Conclusion

It is indisputable that something happens after you die. We will experience a new reality after we die. It is convenient and soul-soothing to believe that the experience will be good. It could be, after all! Nirvana,

---

[18] http://en.wikipedia.org/wiki/Incarceration_in_the_United_States
[19] http://www.plosone.org/article/info%3Adoi%2F10.1371%2Fjournal.pone.0039048

reincarnation, Heaven, Hell, and nothing are all possibilities, but this is not an exhaustive list, because the possibilities are endless, and we have no way of knowing whether our concepts of what happens after death are at all true.

We have all been to funerals and memorials. Family and friends speak of the loved one who will be missed. The pastor or overseer of the event helps the loved ones deal with the trauma of losing a loved one. It is an irresistible temptation to affirm that the person is now in a better place. But of course, no one knows for sure. It just makes people feel better to believe so.

Imagine the viewing of a funeral with an open casket. The tears of family and friends flow over the loss of a teenage boy. Mom describes her memories of when he was a child, and friends would reminisce of the time they wrecked while driving home from a party. The minister nervously practices his lines in the back of the church, trying to avoid saying anything that would touch a nerve and cause more pain to the loved ones.

The beautiful face of the much-loved young man is exposed to his mourners' tears. They weep for the promise he had, and will never fulfill. "He was a good boy," they weep, trembling. Each person walks by, shocked to see how such a beautiful young man, who had been so full of life, could now be dead.

The pastor consoles them. He makes them look forward to seeing him again. "Jim is looking down on us all from Heaven…he is in a better place now," the confident minister calmly and gently insists.

Afterward, the crowd mingles for small talk, cookies, and juice. They hold each other and give condolences. Some congratulate the pastor for the best memorial they have ever attended. The pastor humbly accepts their praise.

But where is the young man? The darkness fades to dim light. While hopeful mourners imagine him in heaven, the young man is in the darkness, experiencing the horrors of punishment! He screams as he pays for his sins.

This goes to show that we just do not know! And more often than not, we opt to believe our preference, engaging in wishful thinking in order to avoid the reality of the afterlife.

No One Knows

"I have a great love and respect for religion, great love and respect for atheism. What I hate is agnosticism, people who do not choose."

—Orson Welles[20]

I have read many atheists, and they get pretty animated. They have not seen God, so they conclude that God does not exist. They feel that God is obligated to show Himself, to prove himself real, in order to merit worship. Moreover, they think that if God does not measure up to their standard, he must not exist.

They believe that, if there were a God, he would ensure the world was a good place. Since the world is in such a bad state, atheists prematurely conclude that God does not exist. Case closed! Furthermore, many of them conclude that anyone who believes in God is a fool.

---

[20] http://www.brainyquote.com/quotes/keywords/atheism.html#uwH2gZrwgLcgRJpW.99

This attitude has not engendered a lot of respect from me, not because atheists disagree with me, but because they are not thinking reasonably.

You have read many quotes from relatively famous people who are adamantly against the concept of the afterlife. They gamble their souls on an intellect guided by preferences rather than fact.

I have strong beliefs about Heaven and Hell. I am not saying I know. I have never been to either place, after all. I have not spent time on the beaches of Heaven or roasted hotdogs over the flames of Hell. Who has? No one on earth has sand in their shorts from Heaven or mustard on their shirt from Hell. No matter how smart you are, you cannot have firsthand knowledge of the truth on these matters during your earthly life.

Maybe we believe what we prefer. Did we get it from Grandma who soothed you with words of consolation? Did she tell you bedtime stories, and that you were good boys and girls who were destined for Heaven? Was the girl I met pretty enough to adopt a new philosophy? Was I born a Mormon or an atheist?

It should not surprise us that we have a limited ability to perceive reality. If it is even possible for us to understand God, time, and the universe, we cannot yet claim that we do. My field of study was mathematics, yet I can't understand many things, and Einstein is over my head.

I read that, in four-dimensional space, it is possible to turn a sphere inside out without cutting the sphere. That is, you could turn a basketball inside out in a four dimensional space without slicing open the skin of the ball. I cannot understand this, even though I watched a Youtube video explaining the concept.[21] Some concepts require an understanding so advanced that most of us do not get it. Some might even require an understanding more advanced than any could claim.

It is possible that God is so. He is more complex than the things we study through science. After all, with science we are only scraping the surface in an effort to understand the workings of God's creation. Contemplating the physical universe is tough enough! So it is ridiculous and arrogant to conclude that we have figured out enough to discern that there is no God. As Creator of our realm, God

---

[21] http://www.youtube.com/watch?v=wO61D9x6lNY

is necessarily outside it. Hence, unless we get information directly from Him, we are terminally in the dark age of ignorance when it comes to His existence and purpose.

Many religious leaders claim that they know about God, His purpose, and what he wants us to do. Maybe they do, and maybe they do not. I know that I do not know. I have chosen a leader to trust, and vested my soul in him. I am not making my choice out of preference or inventing the world the way I wish it would be. However, I have decided, as we all must do.

When someone has vested trust in a certain philosophy or religion, they can seem very bold and assertive. I always think, "How can they be so sure?" I realize we need to cut these people some slack—they are just like us, they are trying to understand these larger questions, and they are excited when they think they have discovered the truth. They have made their estimation and are betting their souls. They only speak what they believe, and are desperate to maintain the stability their belief has provided.

I am just hoping we can strip away our emotions, our cultural biases, and our preferences when we consider whom to trust. We need our whole, uncluttered minds to determine the truth. We need a heart that says, "Whatever the truth is, I'll submit to it!" Without this heart and mindset, we might miss the answers that are right before us.

Chris Cornell understands his limited ability to know, and even so, the lyrics he sings show a desire for truth.

> *What if the one thing that I missed*
> *Was everything I need to pass the test?*
> *And if I fail, what happens then?*
> *Can I still count on you as a friend?*

He calls out to his Creator to help him and cut him slack based on his heartfelt attempt to know and submitting to the truth. Pretty cool! My prayer is that Chris finds the truth and lives it, and that God's mercy will provide for him.

Many Speak

"The more thoroughly I conduct scientific research, the more I believe that science excludes atheism."

—Lord Kelvin[22]

I think that what Lord Kelvin says is self-evident. Science shows the complexity of the universe and rules out chance as the cause of all there is, which leaves us with a universal design and a Designer.

There are so many voices in religion: Bahá'í, Buddhism, Islam, Hinduism, Judaism, Mormonism, Jehovah's Witnesses, and Christianity…you and your friends…we are in the same predicament, trying to figure out what all this is for, and what happens next. We need to remember that there are no enemies—just fellow truth seekers.

I have divided Mormons and Jehovah's Witnesses from Christianity because they hold different beliefs on major

---

[22] http://www.brainyquote.com/quotes/quotes/l/lordkelvin389653.html#KkcW1ZfulURAiisi.99

Christian teachings. I have included Catholics and Protestants under Christianity, because they hold to the major Christian doctrines. Methodists, Episcopalians, Lutherans, and Pentecostals, among other Christian denominations, are also basically Christian.

There are similarities and differences among all religions. In a general sense, they are the same in that they teach what it means to be "good" and explain what happens after death. In most, if you are "good," you will go to a better place after death, and if you are "bad," you will go to a worse place. The definition of "good" and "bad" behaviors change depending on the religion. Christianity adds a twist to this general description; it holds that we need God's forgiveness in order to be "good," and shows how to get it.

All religions have something like Hell and Heaven, but each religion has different concepts of what happens in Hell and Heaven.

In high school, I was on the wrestling team. I would be on the mat and I would hear a roar of voices—a giant static roar from the crowd. My mom's distinctive voice would pierce this static, from time to time. In the foreground were my coaches. There were so many voices, each exclaiming their own direction with great enthusiasm. It takes clarity to focus on the match and listen to the right voice.

We have the same experience when it comes to religion and philosophy. The noise roars, and there are so many voices. Pop culture, news, and schools tell us about reality. It is hard to weed out the truth from this excess of information. Sorting through the different approaches to life and living is one of the purposes of this book. The book is meant to help and guide you to making the most educated decision about whom to trust when it comes to questions of death and the afterlife.

Stuck Trusting Someone

We all die and something happens. We do not have any firsthand knowledge of the truth in this matter. We do not know what happens after we die, although we know what we would like to happen. Many say that they know the answer, but these people who say they know do not agree. So we are caught in a quandary of whom to trust.

There is a Hindu proverb describing why there are so many different religious perspectives:

> A number of blind men came to an elephant. Somebody told them that it was an elephant. The blind men asked, "What is the elephant like?" and they began to touch its body. One of them said: "It is like a pillar." This blind man had only touched its leg. Another man said, "The elephant is like a husking basket." This person had only touched its ears. Similarly, he who touched its trunk or its belly talked of it differently. In the same way, he who has seen the Lord in a

particular way limits the Lord to that alone and thinks that He is nothing else.[23]

This parable shows how we humans approach the issue of God. Each religion has a portion of truth, a different interpretation of the same thing. The proverb does not deny that God exists, but in fact affirms it. We come up with different views of God—none right but none wrong, but all different and none complete. So from a human perspective, it is fair to say that none of us possesses all truth. That is why it is important to listen to one another and explore new ideas.

But more importantly, let's consider how this parable would change if someone who can see describes the elephant to the blind.

We are all blind, and we are looking for someone who sees. It is natural that we come up with religion in response to the great thinkers who have described God to us. Siddhartha Gautama, Mohammad, and Joseph Smith are among these. Some religious leaders had enlightenment,

---

[23] http://en.wikipedia.org/wiki/Blind_men_and_an_elephant

some saw angels, and others claim to be God Himself. But have any of them ever truly seen God? Whom can we trust?

I am not at this point advocating one religious guide over another. For now, let's simply consider what each said about his revelation and how he came to know what he called truth.

I do not trust in blind belief. People who refuse to question, who simply give the party line, are unbearable to me. Often, I hear stories from people about some wild occurrence that justifies their stance on an issue. I ask a few questions and often they are offended that I do not just trust what they are saying. I see others jump in to defend this person's uninformed ideas, because they want to believe that a certain thing is true. This kills me!

We had people getting all worked up about Y2K and the end of the Mayan calendar. There was no basis for believing that these two events would cause the end of the world, yet so many people worried about them, and even created elaborate preparations for these cataclysms. I find it amusing and sad that people have been so concerned about the possibility of the end of the world and do not concern themselves seriously with the afterlife. The afterlife is an indisputable reality for us all, regardless of whether we die of old age or of solar radiation.

We must think! This will help us discover whom we can trust. In order to decide whom to trust, let us look at each of the major religious founders.

Hinduism

Hinduism has no historically recorded founder. It is an ancient religion estimated to have its beginnings in 4,000 BC, although estimates vary. Hinduism started from various cultures that worshipped animals, ancestors, and rocks. Over time, it developed from rudimentary forms of honor and worship to a more or less formal religion. There is such diversity in the practices of this religion that it is hard to generalize much. It now has about 330 million gods.[24]

According to Wikipedia:

> Worship in Hinduism is an act of religious
> devotion usually directed to one or more Hindu

---

[24] http://en.wikipedia.org/wiki/List_of_Hindu_deities

deities. A sense of Bhakti or devotional love is generally invoked. This term is probably a central one in Hinduism. A direct translation from the Sanskrit to English is problematic. Worship takes a multitude of forms depending on community groups, geography and language. There is a flavour of loving and being in love with whatever object or focus of devotion. Worship is not confined to any place of worship, it also incorporates personal reflection, art forms and group. Hindus usually perform worship to achieve some specific end or to integrate the body, the mind and the spirit in order to help the performer evolve into a higher being.[25]

Hinduism has no author, no central original text, a multitude of gods, and various forms of worship and spiritual devotion. Because of this, it is a hard religion to assess in terms of whom to trust.

Buddhism (Siddhartha Gautama)

---

[25] http://en.wikipedia.org/wiki/Worship_in_Hinduism

Siddhartha Gautama was the first Buddha, and the founder of Buddhism. He lived from 563 to 483 BC. During his life, he had a revelation (Buddha means "Enlightened One"), which led to a refined system of ideas, methods, and philosophies to apply toward life in order to achieve a better outcome for the afterlife. These were documented about 400 years after the fact.

Siddhartha Gautama focused on the subject of pain, and came to teach that to minimize pain in life requires minimizing desire. According to him, desire causes life's pain.

Moses

According to the Bible, Moses met with God on Mt. Sinai, where God provided him the Ten Commandments. He also met with God in the Tabernacle, which was a type of temple. In the Tabernacle, Moses was instructed in the other Jewish laws and God's preferred forms of worship and sacrifice.

The Jewish people had a system of laws that, when broken, required death in many cases. Yet in certain circumstances, an animal could take on the lawbreaker's iniquity and die in his place, thus acquitting the guilty party from guilt and condemnation. However, since the destruction of the Tabernacle in 70 AD, Jews have no longer performed sacrifices.

Jews also claim that their prophesies indicate the coming of a Messiah, liberator, or savior, who would establish his Kingdom in Jerusalem.

They still wait.

Jesus

The first followers of Jesus were Jews who believed him to be the Messiah. Most Jews did not believe he was the Messiah, yet many did recognize him as a great prophet. Today, he is generally considered by the Jews to be an apostate—a traitor.

He claimed to be the incarnation of God. In the scriptures, he was called Emmanuel, meaning "God with us." The name Jesus means, "Savior of his people."

It was prophesied that the Messiah would die on the cross to redeem the sins of all the individuals of the world. He prophesied that he would raise himself from the dead, and his followers claim that he did. Following his resurrection, he spent forty days on earth with his followers; over five hundred followers claimed to have seen him.

His disciples all were killed (except Apostle John, who died in prison) for proclaiming that Jesus had risen from the dead. They admonished people everywhere to obey Jesus's command that we live lives of sacrificial love.

He performed many miracles before large crowds. The Jewish historian Josephus, who worked for the Roman government that ruled over Judea, asserted that Jesus existed and did perform miracles.[26]

Mohammad

---

[26] http://en.wikipedia.org/wiki/Josephus_on_Jesus

Would you believe that Mohammad saw an angel also? He was born in Mecca, in 570 AD. It is said that the angel Gabriel gave the words of the Koran to Mohammad, which he memorized and taught to his followers. These words were not recorded in writing by his followers until about one hundred years after Mohammad's death.

Judaism and Christianity pre-date Islam. Judaism and Christianity had spread through the Middle East and North Africa by the time Islam was formed. Mohammad lived in areas where Christians and Jews lived.

The Koran refers to the Bible as a true document. It mentions many Biblical characters, including Jesus. Islamists consider Mohammad to be the paraclete. Mohammad stated that he felt he was the fulfillment of Jesus's promise to send another.

Bahá'í (Bahá'u'lláh)

The Bahá'í religion was born in Persia (Iran) in a Muslim context in the mid-1800s. Bahá'u'lláh has a wild story, which is interesting to look into if you want to learn more than the brief history I will provide here. Wikipedia.com is a great source.

Babi' lived in the early 1800s and claimed to be the prophesied redeemer of Islam. He began what was called the Babi' movement in Persia.

After Babi' was executed, Bahá'u'lláh took over the religion, although not immediately. The Babi's—those who followed the self-proclaimed redeemer Babi'—attempted to kill the Shah of Persia. Many Babi's were killed and imprisoned as a result of this attempt. One of these, Bahá'u'lláh, said he saw an angel while he was imprisoned, and that the angel gave him instructions. Bahá'u'lláh later wrote down the code of this new religion.

Bahá'u'lláh claimed that he was the paraclete. Paraclete means helper, counselor, and consoler. This concept is from Christianity, as Jesus said he would send another, the paraclete. In the New Testament, the Helper was the Spirit of God, who fell upon the disciples of Jesus at Pentecost, a traditional Jewish feast. Through the disciples of Jesus, the paraclete performed powerful miracles as documented in the book of Acts in the New Testament.

Bahá'u'lláh's followers consider him, rather than the Spirit of God, to be the paraclete sent by Jesus.

[Bahá'u'lláh's] verses were very popular among Muslim apologists, who saw in them a prediction of Muhammad's coming. On the one hand, Bahá'u'lláh confirmed that Jesus gave them glad-tidings of a prophet who would come after him, appearing to confirm that Muhammad was the paraclete. On the other hand, in Bahá'u'lláh's cyclical schema of the Eternal Return, the Counsellor would come again and again, first as Muhammad, then as the Bab (Bahá'u'lláh). This figure becomes another way of referring to the spiritual return of Christ.[27]

Joseph Smith

Joseph Smith was an American born in Vermont, but he also saw an angel. He wrote *The Book of Mormon* at the age of twenty-four years. He claimed that an angel directed him to golden plates written in an unknown language, and

---

[27] http://bahai-library.com/cole_behold_man

that he used seer stones to translate these plates, which became *The Book of Mormon*.

> According to Latter Day Saint history, seer stones were stones used, primarily (but not exclusively) by Joseph Smith Jr, to receive revelations from God.
>
> Smith owned at least two seer stones, which he had earlier employed for treasure seeking before he founded the church. Other early Mormons such as Hiram Page, David Whitmer, and Jacob Whitmer also owned seer stones. Seer stones are mentioned in the Book of Mormon and in other Latter Day Saint scriptures. James Strang, who claimed to be Joseph Smith's designated successor, also unearthed what he said were ancient metal plates and translated them using seer stones.[28]

Although Mormons define themselves as a Christian sect, they differ greatly on major doctrines of the historic

---

[28] http://en.wikipedia.org/wiki/Seer_stone_%28Latter_Day_Saints%29

Christian Faith. They believe that Satan is Jesus's brother. It is their belief that a Mormon believer will become a god of his own planet after death. These are ideas that cannot be found in the texts upon which the Christian religion has been based.

Charles Taze Russell

Charles T. Russell was the founder of the Watch Tower and the Jehovah's Witness in the late 1800s. Their translation of the Bible is called *The New World Translation*, and was published in 1950. This translation of the Bible significantly differs from other translations of the Bible, and Christians do not accept it as a legitimate translation. Jehovah's Witnesses have derived doctrines from this translation that differ greatly from those of traditional Christianity. For one thing, they do not believe that Jesus was God incarnate.

This religion is similar to Mormonism in that both were formed in the 1800s in the United States, both claim to be a reformed type of Christianity, and both differ significantly from the beliefs of Christianity.

Summary

"The easy confidence with which I know another man's religion is folly teaches me to suspect that my own is also."
—Mark Twain[29]

If someone came to you and said, "I saw an angel," what would you think? What if someone said "I have a great idea about what life is all about"? What would you do? Most of us would think, "Who is this guy? Why should I trust him?"

How would you determine whether to trust him or not? Would you believe his strange words because you like him or like what he said? Would you disqualify him if the ramifications of his ideas would deeply impact your life? What if you would have to change?

Your honest answers to these questions will indicate that many of our aversions to a particular idea have nothing to do with truth, but rather pivot on our fears and the ramifications of this truth on our lives. However, we

---
[29] http://coolquotescollection.com/Religious/11

must not consider reactions based on biases and fears to indicate whether or not something is true. In fact, these are the enemies of truth.

A smoker does not like the fact that smoking may cause cancer and other health complications. Quitting will reduce the smoker's chance of getting cancer, but the drive to smoke overrides the facts. Even though smoking is irrational and potentially destructive behavior, the smoker buries the fact deep in his mind in order to permit continued smoking. He does not believe the facts, but instead believes his preference. "Maybe I will beat the odds!" he thinks.

This approach is no different from how most people treat religion. As the smoker is addicted to nicotine, so are we addicted to the lives we have designed. Even though these lives may be cataclysmic, even though they may cause us eternal pain, we persist because we prefer to believe we will be the exception to the rule. We procrastinate quitting our habit in order to achieve short-term pleasure, at risk to our long-term well-being.

Even after looking at all this information on religion, we will not come up with an absolute truth so very factual as cancer rates in smokers. Nonetheless, we still must choose what we believe about death and the afterlife. Instead of facts, we are left to work with probabilities. As I have already mentioned, we make most of our decisions on important aspects of our life by considering whom we trust and the probability that a certain event will happen as we hope.

One example is marriage. Most of us want to be married for life to the same person. If we find a person whom we like, whom we trust, with whom we have things in common, and with whom we share similar goals and ideas about marriage and family, we often join in marriage. Time will tell if we chose wisely!

So it is with these religious founders. You must ask yourself: whom can I most probably trust? The answer matters! You have only one chance to get it right. According to some religions, this life is the only opportunity you have.

Making no decision on this matter is still a choice with consequences. If you decide you can trust none of them, then you simply trust yourself. But how can you trust yourself when you know absolutely nothing about the afterlife? It is foolish to trust yourself when you do not have firsthand knowledge. Would you trust yourself to perform surgery just because you don't trust the doctor?

Following a certain leader requires trusting his expertise. Which one of these can we trust? Whom do we think we can trust and why?

Jesus in Religion

It would be remiss of me not to mention that Jesus is referenced in all religions as a great teacher, a Holy man, a prophet, a god, the Son of God, or God himself. Naturally, the newly formed American religions (Mormonism and Jehovah's Witnesses) are centered around him. Each claim to be a Christian religion, a reconstructed true Church, so of course Christ would be a central figure for them.

Furthermore, Jesus is mentioned often in the Koran. Like Christians, Mormons, and Jehovah's Witnesses, the Koran holds that its religion (Islam) is the fulfillment of the true religion of the Jews and Christians.

Eastern religions also refer to Jesus. Bahá'í, Buddhism, and Hinduism have great respect for him, even though the roots of Buddhism and Hinduism predate Christianity.

Jesus is the only world religious leader to be co-opted by all other religions, while the leaders of other religions were not readily accepted by the other religions and certainly are not universally acknowledged. Buddhists do not exalt Joseph Smith, and the Jehovah's Witness do not recognize Mohammad as a prophet. This might be our first clue. But to make sure, we will look at some of the references that other religions make to Jesus.

Mohammad

Jesus is referenced twenty-eight times by name in the Koran.[30] A Muslim, speaking to a Christian audience, once noted that the name of Jesus is mentioned five times more often than Mohammad's name is written in the Koran.[31]

The Koran holds:

> When Jesus came with Clear Signs, he said: "Now I have come to you with Wisdom, and in order to make clear to you some of the (points) on which you dispute. Therefore, fear God and obey me. God, He is my Lord and your Lord, so worship Him—this is a Straight Way." But sects from among themselves fell into disagreement. So woe

---

[30] http://wiki.answers.com/Q/How_many_times_is_the_name_Jesus_mentioned_in_the_quran
[31] http://youtu.be/PTLrZFJ0KOg

to the wrongdoers, from the penalty of a Grievous Day![32]

Included in the Koran's teachings about Jesus are the following ideas:

> Different texts in the Qur'an...point to Jesus as being in a special class of prophet, a class that Mohammed himself does not seem to attain. For instance, the Qur'an testifies to the following regarding Jesus:
> - Jesus was born a virgin (Surah 3:45–50).
> - Jesus is sinless (Surah 6:85).
> - Jesus is the Messiah (Surah 3:45).
> - Jesus performed miracles (Surah 3:49).
>
> One of these miracles is especially interesting (although only attested elsewhere in the Gospel of Thomas). Surah 3:49 and 5:110 teach that Jesus created a bird out of clay while He was upon this earth.
> - Jesus ascended into heaven in bodily form (Surah 3:55).
> - Jesus spoke at his birth (Surah 19:27–35).

---

[32] Sura 43:63-65

- Jesus raised the dead (Surah 3:49).[33]

The Koran takes a very high view of Jesus, claiming that he was sinless, was the Messiah, and performed many miracles. In addition, the Koran says Jesus will come again as the Bible has prophesied.

Joseph Smith

The Mormon religion uses Jesus's name in their very title: The Church of Jesus Christ of Latter-day Saints. Jesus is mentioned hundreds of times in the Book of Mormon. In fact, they hold that Jesus visited the Americas following the resurrection. Their book is intended to be a companion to the Christian Bible.

Mormons believe that Jesus is a Son of God who created the Earth, and that Jesus redeems His people through His substitutionary death on the cross. They often speak using the same terms as orthodox Christianity, while having different meanings for these terms. This can make

---

[33] http://seeingclearly.wordpress.com/2009/02/21/what-does-the-quran-teach-about-jesus/

it confusing for the layperson to differentiate between the two.

According to official Mormon teaching, Jesus Christ is the first spirit child conceived and begotten by Heavenly Father and one of Heavenly Father's many wives (commonly referred to as "Heavenly Mother"). Just as Heavenly Father before him progressed to godhood, so Jesus progressed through obedience to the status of a god (prior to his incarnation on earth). In the words of the late Mormon Apostle and General Authority Bruce McConkie, Jesus Christ through obedience and devotion "attained that pinnacle of intelligence which ranked him as a God." As such, according to LDS authorities, Jesus is not to be worshiped or prayed to as one would worship or pray to Heavenly Father.

Furthermore, Mormons teach that Heavenly Father subsequently had other spirit children. We ourselves are thought to be spirit children of Father God and Mother God. As such, Mormons refer to Jesus as our "Elder brother." As the official LDS teacher's manual Gospel Principles explains, "We needed a Savior to pay for our sins and teach us how to return to our Heavenly Father. Our Father said, 'Whom shall I send?' (Abraham 3:27). Two of our brothers offered to help. Our oldest brother, Jesus Christ, who was then called Jehovah, said, "Here am I, send me." [34]

In this way, Jesus is central to their religion. I say this because, while they reference him and say that they follow the Bible, their primary point of reference is *The Book of Mormon* as provided by Joseph Smith, which gives a certain spin on their understanding of Jesus. They also have developed new ceremonies and doctrines from this point of view that are foreign to traditional Christianity.

Watchtower

Much like the Mormon Church, the Watchtower was established in the nineteenth century in the United States. Their teachings are different from the Christian teaching

---

[34] http://www.equip.org/bible_answers/does-mormonism-really-teach-that-jesus-is-the-spirit-brother-of-satan/

that has been established for over two millennia all over the world.

Their general belief about Jesus and Christianity is as follows:

1. Jesus Christ is not God. Rather, he is Michael the archangel.
2. The Holy Spirit is not a person, but an "active force." J.W.s are unitarians, denying the Trinity.
3. When you're dead, you're dead. Man has no eternal soul, any more than animals.
4. Jesus Christ was not raised bodily from the grave, but was recreated as a new "spirit body."
5. Jesus returned invisibly in 1914. There is no "visible coming" planned in the future.
6. There is no hell. Just like animals, when we die, it is over.
7. Only 144,000 people achieve heaven. The rest, faithful Witnesses who have died, will be recreated on earth during the kingdom of the "New World."

Focusing on the Old Testament, their system is a legalistic one. They forbid blood transfusions (they say that is eating blood). They also consider any salute to a flag as worship of that flag, and therefore prohibited. They don't vote, hold public office or serve in the military.[35]

These main discrepancies show the vast differences between orthodox Christianity and Jehovah's Witness.

Hinduism

It is not surprising that Muslims, Bahá'ís, Mormons, and Jehovah's Witnesses refer to and elevate Jesus and His teachings, as they all began after the advent of Christianity. It comes as a surprise to most of us to learn that religions like Hinduism and Buddhism reference Jesus, since they pre-date Christianity. However, prominent Hindus have referred to Jesus in the following ways:

> In my particular tradition, and among other Hindus, He [Jesus] is seen as much more, as an Avatar, specifically a Shaktavesha Avatar or an

---

[35] http://www.chick.com/bc/1985/jehovahswitness.asp

empowered incarnation. This means that God has sent Him to us for a specific mission to fulfill God's will on earth.[36]

I regard Jesus as a great teacher of humanity, but I do not regard him as the only begotten son of God. That epithet in its material interpretation is quite unacceptable. Metaphorically we are all sons of God, but for each of us there may be different sons of God in a special sense. Thus for me Chaitanya may be the only begotten son of God . . . God cannot be the exclusive Father and I cannot ascribe exclusive divinity to Jesus.[37]

I came to the conclusion long ago . . . that all religions were true and also that all had some error in them, and whilst I hold by my own, I should hold others as dear as Hinduism. So we can only pray, if we are Hindus, not that a Christian should become a Hindu . . . . But our

---

[36] http://www.bbc.co.uk/religion/religions/hinduism/beliefs/jesus_1.shtml
[37] Harijan: June 3, 1937

innermost prayer should be a Hindu should be a better Hindu, a Muslim a better Muslim, a Christian a better Christian.[38]

"Jesus occupies in my heart," said Gandhi, "the place of one of the greatest teachers who have had a considerable influence on my life. I shall say to the Hindus that your life will be incomplete unless you reverentially study the teachings of Jesus. . . . Make this world the kingdom of God and his righteousness and everything will be added unto you. I tell you that if you will understand, appreciate, and act up to the spirit of this passage, you won't need to know what place Jesus or any other teacher occupies in your heart."[39]

Wow! You might think that Hindus were Christians, given their respect for Jesus.

---

[38] Young India: January 19, 1928
[39] http://robtshepherd.tripod.com/gandhi.html

Buddhism

Jesus was born hundreds of years after the advent of Buddhism. So of course the religion formally has nothing to say about him. However, much has been said about his relationship to Buddhism since. Some call him a Buddha or reincarnation of the original Buddha, Siddhartha Gautama. Others postulate that Jesus went to India when he was a child, and perhaps absorbed some Eastern philosophy there, although there is no reliable historical documentation or mention of this in the New Testament.

An interview with the Dalai Lama shows his great respect for Jesus:

Q: Do you ever experience rages? Even Jesus had rages.

A: Don't compare me with Jesus. He is a great master, a great master. But as to your question, when I was younger, I did get angry. In the past thirty years, no. One thing, the hatred, the ill-feeling, that's almost gone.

Bahá'í

The Bahá'ís have a high view of Jesus as well. According to the Bahá'í, "The Christian monarchs were also asked to be faithful to Jesus's call to follow the promised 'Spirit of Truth.'"[40]

The following are some worthwhile quotes that show how Bahá'ís lift Jesus to a high place in humanity.

The Bible and the Gospels are most honored in the estimation of all Bahá'ís. One of the spiritual utterances of His Holiness Christ in his Sermon on the Mount is preferable to me to all the writings of the philosophers. It is the religious duty of every Bahá'í to read and comprehend the meanings of the Old and New Testament.[41]

In summary, the Bahá'í scriptures do not reject the uniqueness of Jesus Christ; on the

---

[40] http://en.wikipedia.org/wiki/Bah%C3%A1%27u%27ll%C3%A1h
[41] Abdu'l-Baha, Star of the West, Vol. 14, p. 55

contrary, they respect, love, and emphasize it.

However, they seek to balance that uniqueness by recognizing the uniqueness of other Manifestations of God as well. This balance is achieved by seeing Manifestations as perfect expressions of the divine will for the people of their place and time. The Manifestations bring eternal and unchanging religious teachings to the people as well as principles designed for the society to which they minister. Thus Jesus is seen by Bahá'ís as divine, as the Son of Man and the Son of God, and as the way, truth, and life to His world. Ironically, this is more than many Christians believe about Jesus. The Bahá'í view of the station of Jesus falls near the middle of the spectrum of views that Christians hold, and claims to understand Jesus in a way fitting to our modern, pluralistic, and historically-minded world.[42]

---

[42] http://bahai-library.com/stockman_jesus_bahai_writings

Judaism

Some Jews of Jesus's time viewed him as their prophesied Messiah and became His first followers. Thus, the first Christians were initially Jews. Furthermore, many Jews considered him a prophet, but did not believe he was the Messiah.

Today, most Jews deny even that he was a prophet, and many even believe that he was a false Jewish teacher. There are thus some mixed feelings among Jewish peoples when it comes to the teachings of Christ.

> From my youth onwards I have found in Jesus my great brother. That Christianity has regarded and does regard him as God and Savior has always appeared to me a fact of the highest importance which, for his sake and my own, I must endeavor to understand ... I am more than ever certain that a great place belongs to him in Israel's history of faith and that this place cannot be described by any of the usual categories.[43]

---

[43] Martin Buber, leading Jewish writer, thinker, philosopher, and theologian (1878-1965). http://www.jewishvoice.org/who-is-yeshua/quotes-about-jesus/

Benjamin Disraeli, who became Britain's prime minister, articulated Christianity's dependence on Judaism:

"In all church discussions we are apt to forget the second Testament is avowedly only a supplement. Jesus came to complete the law and the prophets. Christianity is completed Judaism or it is nothing. Christianity is incomprehensible without Judaism, as Judaism is incomplete without Christianity."[44]

New Testament Jews and modern Jews have quite different views on Jesus. It is interesting to note that the Jewish people have alternately rejected and accepted many Jewish prophets as time passed. They have killed and persecuted quite a few of their prophets, and then accepted them posthumously. Nevertheless, many Jews have come to yield to Jesus over the centuries.

Summary

Every major religion points to Jesus. On one hand, it is amazing that all religions but Judaism exalt Jesus, and

---

[44] Benjamin Disraeli, Prime Minister of England
http://www.jewishvoice.org/who-is-yeshua/quotes-about-jesus/

recognize not only his wisdom, but also his holiness. They support his divine origin and mandate. They recognize that he is the highest model for life. On the other hand, maybe it is not surprising that they all point to Jesus. He was an outstanding individual who affected many lives.

Consider the example of Keith Green, born in Brooklyn, New York, in 1953. He was a musical prodigy noted for his talent by the age of eight years old. He had a Jewish heritage and was raised a Christian Scientist. However, he left his parents' religion and began seeking truth in Eastern mysticism.[45]

After some time, Keith discovered that Eastern religions all pointed back to Jesus. He and his wife (who was also of Jewish heritage) came to recognize Jesus as Messiah and began to follow the way of Jesus. Keith went on to create a great stir in Christianity as a Christian reformer.

---

[45] http://en.wikipedia.org/wiki/Keith_Green

Worst-Case Analysis

Let us consider these religions from an exceedingly practical perspective by conducting a worst-case analysis. A worst-case analysis is the process of determining the worst possible scenario and developing a plan to avoid it.

Safety nets are important when the stakes are high. Consider the context of rock climbing. For an easy climb well within the climber's capabilities—say, only a few feet from the ground, the climber would not require the protection of ropes and harnesses. It would become necessary to use protection if this easy climb were performed on a thousand foot cliff, however. The consequences of a fall from this height call for great care to be taken in order to avoid such a fall.

In the same way, it is important to consider the afterlife and protect yourself against danger. Who would climb at a thousand-feet high without protection just to have more fun time climbing? Take this perspective with you when it comes to your soul, and take precautions to avoid terrible punishment in the afterlife.

How do we avoid punishment after death? In order to avoid punishment after death, whose guidance would we trust?

All of the religions, except that of the Jehovah's Witnesses, teach a type of punishment in the afterlife, although descriptions of the experience and duration of suffering differ. In some cases, the guilty are eventually released to Paradise. But all contain the idea that the "wicked" will be castigated after death. Below is described each religion's form of punishment and their directions on how to evade it. This will help us to determine what the worst-case scenario is and how to avoid it.

Living in denial will not change the truth. If Hell exists, pretending, stamping your feet, and arguing against it will not change the fact. So let us think rationally about how to proceed in our lives.

Bahá'í

In Bahá'í, the punishment for wickedness after death is being placed at a long distance from God. If you're really good, the reward is to be closer in proximity to the presence of God. Their punishment for the sins of this life is analogous to getting bad tickets to a show that you love. In order to avoid punishment, all you have to do is be "good."

> In the final analysis, heaven can be seen partly as a state of nearness to God; hell is a state of remoteness from God. Each state follows as a natural consequence of individual efforts, or the lack thereof, to develop spiritually. The key to spiritual progress is to follow the path outlined by the Manifestations of God.[46]

Buddhism

In Buddhism, the evil are punished after death in a place called Narakas, which is a cavernous place of torment under the Earth. It is not eternal. Karma determines when one will be released from Narakas. Upon release, Karma

---

[46] http://info.bahai.org/article-1-4-5-2.html

determines what level of reincarnation one experiences. To avoid punishment, all you have to do is be "good."

> Physically, Narakas are thought of as a series of cavernous layers which extend below Jambudvīpa (the ordinary human world) into the earth. There are several schemes for enumerating these Narakas and describing their torments. The Abhidharma-kosa (Treasure House of Higher Knowledge) is the root text that describes the most common scheme, the Eight Cold Narakas and Eight Hot Narakas.[47]

Judaism

Judaism has a temporary Hell. The guilty are punished in Hell for twelve months, and then released to Heaven. If one is still not worthy of Heaven after twelve months, the soul might cease to exist or might be eternally punished; there is dispute over this amongst Jews. To avoid

---

[47] http://en.wikipedia.org/wiki/Naraka_%28Buddhism%29

punishment, all you have to do is be "good." In this case, to be good means to follow the Law of Moses and be charitable.

> The soul's sentence in Gehinnom is usually limited to a twelve-month period of purgation before it takes its place in Olam Ha-Ba (Mishnah Eduyot 2:9, Shabbat 33a). This twelve-month limit is reflected in the yearlong mourning cycle and the recitation of the Kaddish (the memorial prayer for the dead). Only the utterly wicked do not ascend to Gan Eden at the end of this year. Sources differ on what happens to these souls at the end of their initial time of purgation. Some say that the wicked are utterly destroyed and cease to exist, while others believe in eternal damnation.[48]

Jehovah's Witness

The punishment for earthly sins in the Jehovah's Witness religion is annihilation. To avoid punishment, all

---

[48] http://www.myjewishlearning.com/beliefs/Theology/Afterlife_and_Messiah/Life_After_Death/Heaven_and_Hell.s html

you have to do is be a Jehovah's Witness and follow their practices.

> They totally deny the existence of the traditional Christian view of Hell. Satan is regarded as having created the concept of Hellfire in order to turn people against God. They believe that hell is the "common grave of mankind" where people go when they die. They are not conscious there. Unbelievers simply cease to exist at death. Believers remain in death until the resurrection.[49]

Mormonism

The Mormons believe that punishment for earthly sins occurs is in a type of prison for souls called the Outer Darkness. After the thousand-year reign of Christ on Earth (a future prophesied event of the Bible), some souls in the Outer Darkness (another name for Hell) will be resurrected and permitted to enter the lowest level of Heaven. The very wicked and unrepentant will go back to

---

[49] http://www.towerwatch.com/Witnesses/Beliefs/their_beliefs.htm

the Outer Darkness forever. To avoid punishment, all you have to do is be "good." Those who are not Mormons but are "good" people will go to heaven, albeit a low level of heaven. To enter the high heaven, you need to be a practicing Mormon.

On this same subject Bruce McConkie (a member of the Quorum of the Twelve Apostles of Latter Day Saints: Mormonism) explained:

"When the wicked depart this life, they are 'cast out into outer darkness,' into hell, where 'they have no part nor portion of the Spirit of the Lord,' where they are spiritually dead."[50]

Currently hell in spirit prison is a holding tank for the souls of the wicked. Here they remain until the end of the millennium when they will be resurrected and judged. Those with crimes not including murder or apostasy will be allowed entrance into the telestial kingdom, which is the lowest of the kingdoms of glory. Those who failed

---

[50] (Alma 40:13-14.) http://www.mrm.org/heaven-and-hell

to prove themselves worthy of a telestial reward will return again to outer darkness, this time for eternity.[51]

Islam

The Hell of Islam is like that of Christianity. Punishment is eternal, with no escape. In Islam:

Hell, or Jahannam (Greek gehenna), is mentioned frequently in the Qur'an and the Sunnah using a variety of imagery. It has seven doors (Qur'an 39:71; 15:43) leading to a fiery crater of various levels, the lowest of which contains the tree Zaqqum and a cauldron of boiling pitch. The level of hell depends on the degree of offenses. Suffering is both physical and spiritual.[52]

Those who are not Muslims following the Five Pillars of Islam will go to Hell.

---

[51] http://www.mrm.org/heaven-and-hell
[52] http://www.religionfacts.com/islam/beliefs/afterlife.htm

The Koran is inconsistent on the issue of the afterlife for those who practice Judaism and Christianity. In some chapters, Christians and Jews will go to Heaven; other chapters state that they will go to Hell. For the sake of preparedness, we will assume the more restrictive case for this analysis: that Jews and Christians go to Hell. To avoid punishment, all you have to do is obey Allah as prescribed by the Five Pillars of Islam. These are:

1. To accept the *shahada* (Islamic creed), that there is no God but Allah and Mohammad is His messenger.
2. To conduct daily prayers (*salah*) five times a day.
3. To give alms (*zakāt*) to the poor at a rate of 2.5% of your income.
4. To fast during the day (*sawm*) in the month of Ramadan, which lasts forty days.
5. To conduct a pilgrimage to Mecca (*hajj*) at least once in a lifetime. [53]

Hinduism

---

[53] http://en.wikipedia.org/wiki/Five_Pillars_of_Islam

In Hinduism, there are twenty-eight hells. After death, one is given a body that is able to withstand the torments of hell, and is then eventually released to re-start the cycle of reincarnation.

Needless to say, hell is not a comfortable place to live in. However, the situation is not hopeless. After finishing its term in hell, the soul is re-sent to earth in any one of the 8.4 million life-forms. It may be given the body of an insect, bird, tree or an animal. Then, based on the devotion it has performed in innumerable past lifetimes, the soul one day becomes deserving of the most desirable form: the human form.[54]

Christianity

Christians believe that Hell is eternal punishment without escape. To avoid Hell, one needs to obey Jesus. Through this trust in Jesus, one's iniquities are forgiven.

---

[54] http://radhamadhavsociety.org/teachings/heaven-and-hell.aspx

According to Jesus's words in the New Testament, "Anyone who says, 'You fool!' will be in danger of the fire of hell."[55]

He goes on to say:

And if your right hand causes you to sin, cut it off and throw it away. It is better for you to lose one part of your body than for your whole body to go into hell.[56]

Some will not be redeemed. There is no doctrine which I would more willingly remove from Christianity than this if it lay in my power.[57]

Dante's *Inferno* indicates the seriousness of Hell in the described inscription that marks Hell's gates: "Abandon hope, all ye who enter here!"[58]

---

[55] Matthew 5:22
http://www.religionfacts.com/christianity/beliefs/hell.htm
[56] Matthew 5:29. See parallel passage in Mark 9:44, which adds, "Where the fire never goes out."
http://www.religionfacts.com/christianity/beliefs/hell.htm
[57] C.S. Lewis, *The Problem of Pain*
http://www.religionfacts.com/christianity/beliefs/hell.htm
[58] http://www.religionfacts.com/christianity/beliefs/hell.htm

According to early church leaders, "The way of darkness is crooked, and it is full of cursing. It is the way of eternal death with punishment."[59]

Furthermore, they held:

> You should fear what is truly death, which is reserved for those who will be condemned to the eternal fire. It will afflict those who are committed to it even to the end.[60]

Summary

People can be defined by their adherence to one of four ways to guide behavior in life. These four types of people can be called the Liberated, the Pragmatist, the Moralist, and the Religious.

The Liberated want to live unhindered by social mores, and do only what they desire.

---

[59] (Pseudo-Barnabas, c. 70-130 AD)
http://www.religionfacts.com/christianity/beliefs/hell.htm
[60] (Letter to Diognetus, c. 125-200)
http://www.religionfacts.com/christianity/beliefs/hell.htm

The Pragmatist is similar, but has greater awareness of consequences. This is a person who isn't too good or too bad. He determines good or bad by the risks and potential gains of his behaviors. It is not that he does not have morality, but that morality is given equal footing with cultural expectations, personal loss/gain, and the possible outcomes of the circumstances. An example of a Pragmatist is a person who lies on his taxes because it is unlikely he will be audited by the IRS.

The Moralist almost always does well. He enjoys being kind and above-the-board in his dealings. He avoids conflict and enjoys that others perceive him as being good.

The Religious have chosen a certain religion and follow its tenets. They consider themselves to be good people, from a human, cultural, and religious standpoint.

The worst-case analysis chart below indicates the worst-case scenario for each of the people described above, according to the various religions described in this book.

Worst-Case Analysis Chart

Type	J. W.	Bahá'í	Bud	Hind	Juda	Morm	Islam	Christ
Liberated	Xn	Xd	Xa	Xa	Xa	Xa	X	X
Pragmatist	Xn	†	†	†	†	†	X	X
Moralist	Xn	†	†	†	†	†	X	X
Religious	Xn	†	†	†	†	†	X	X

X = Eternal Punishment; Xa = Punishment, with possible release; Xd = Large distance from God; Xn = Annihilation; † = No Punishment

Those who want to live a liberated life are in trouble with every religion. No matter which religion is true, they will suffer punishment. The only hope they have is if Buddhism, Hinduism, Judaism, or Mormonism is true, in which case they might be saved from punishment. If the Jehovah's Witnesses are right, the Liberated would not be in bad shape after death—they simply would cease to exist, with the rest of us who choose not to follow the Jehovah's Witness.

The Pragmatists, Moralists, and Religious need not worry about punishment in the view of Buddhism, Hinduism, or Bahá'í. They can live the quasi-good-life and be fine. All that is required is that they be "good" to avoid punishment in the afterlife. According to these religions, the Religious have no advantage over the Pragmatists.

They will live a good life like a Pragmatist, and there may be little difference in their morality. Religion may only be an asset in motivating one to be good. Like the Pragmatist, the Religious will not be punished under most religious philosophies.

However, with the more exclusive religions (Islam, Christianity, and Jehovah's Witness), if one chooses the correct religion and adheres to its teaching, then he may be delivered from the punishment prescribed by their religion. That is, if Islam is true, a good Muslim will gain Heaven. However, it would not help to be a Muslim if the Jehovah's Witness or Christianity were true. These three religions are exclusive; if you do not follow their way, you cannot receive a heavenly reward. It does not matter how "good" you have been—if you did not follow the precepts of the particular religion, you will be punished (or annihilated, in the case of the Jehovah's Witness). In this case, the religion defines "good" above and beyond culture and social norms. If you follow the particular religion, then you are "good."

Since this is a worst case analysis that considers eternal punishment to be the worst possible outcome, the punishment of the Jehovah's Witness isn't considered to be among the worst case, even though Jehovah's Witness believe that they exclusively have hope for a rewarded afterlife. Not existing is not as harsh as eternal torment—in fact, it might be kind of a relief!

Ultimately, if Bahá'í, Hinduism, Buddhism, or Mormonism is true, then your religion is irrelevant so long as you are a good person. You could even be agnostic or atheist, so long as you are "good." In this case, "All good dogs go to Heaven," or reincarnate in an improved state. At the least, I guess we can hope for this. Still, it is wiser to follow the adage, "Hope for the best and prepare for the worst!"

Therefore, the most concerning religions in this analysis are Islam and Christianity. Assuming that eternal punishment is the worst possible outcome, the Xs in the chart above indicate that it is possible for all four types of people to suffer the worst punishment when it comes to Islam and Christianity. Therefore, Islam and Christianity especially need our attention, as we are considering how to protect ourselves from the worst possible afterlife scenario. They are both exclusive and threaten Hell for not following! We should do all we can to avoid going to Hell.

If one chooses Islam or Christianity, and one of the others are true, the worst thing that would happen is annihilation. (And in the best case, one would still go to Heaven or go up the chain of reincarnation on the way to a good place.) However, if one chooses one of the other religions and Islam or Christianity happens to be true, then eternal punishment is the outcome.

Consequently, from a worst-case scenario perspective, it would be safest to adhere to Islam or Christianity in order to avoid potential punishment in Hell.

This analysis assumes that we have no idea what is true and we are only concerned about avoiding Hell. It also assumes that one of the religions is right while the others are wrong.

So, we are left with Islam and Christianity as our best protection against eternal punishment. But which to choose? They both attest the same end to those who do not adhere to their religion and practices. And they are both distinctly different.

At this point, you go back to probability. Which is most likely true?

The easiest way to determine which is most likely true is to look at the two origin texts. Since the Bible precedes the Koran, the Koran references the Bible to legitimize itself. The Koran states that its authenticity can be verified in the Bible. It says that the Koran agrees that the Bible is true. Thus, it states, "I believe in the Book (of the People of the Book) which God has sent down."[61] The People of the Book are understood to be Jews and Christians; the Koran uses the word "Book" to reference the Bible.

There are more Suras in the Koran that confirm the Bible to be true, such as, "To thee we sent the scripture (Qur'an) in truth confirming the scripture that came before it, and guarding it in safety"[62] and "If thou are in doubt as to what We have revealed, then ask the People of the Book."[63]

However, the fact that the Koran bases its authenticity on the Bible causes a problem for the Koran, because it differs in a variety of ways from the Bible, including its

---

[61] *The Noble Qur'an, 42:15.* http://www.answering-christianity.com/mucahit_sivri/quran_and_gospel.htm
[62] The Noble Qur'an, 5:48
[63] *The Noble Qur'an, 10:94* http://www.answering-christianity.com/mucahit_sivri/quran_and_gospel.htm

telling of the stories of the Old Testament and certain important facts.[64]

Thus, the Koran is self-refuting. It says that the Bible will validate its veracity, but the Bible does not. It is as though a teenager says to a policeman, "Ask my mom if I smoke marijuana!" and to the poor kid's surprise, Mom tells the cops how much!

Islam states that the Bible is true. But, because the Bible is different from Islam on several key facts and stories, then the Koran proves its own duplicity. It does not live up to the standard of veracity it has set. This is one more reason to choose Jesus as your guide to heaven.

If it were simply a matter of not going to Hell, a worst-case analysis is a great tool for helping you to choose whom to follow. The safety first approach indicates that you should choose Jesus.

---

[64] http://answering-islam.org/BehindVeil/btv7.html

The Odds

I was always root for the underdog. When I watch football I usually go against the odds. I think it is because I like the overcomer, the unlikely hero. But this is all for fun, a great diversion. But in the case of the afterlife I do not gamble, I go with the odds.

The Jews were waiting for their redeemer under Roman occupation when Jesus was born. The Old Testament—the Jewish religious text—spoke of his coming and described the many prophesies that he would fulfill. For thousands of years, writers of the Bible described the Savior who was to come. They told of His race, where he would live, where he would be born, and many other facts about the Messiah's future life and death.

Jesus fulfilled many ancient prophesies of the Old Testament. His fulfillment of these prophesies indicates that he was the Savior sent by God to redeem mankind.

Could He have purposely fulfilled the prophecies so as to make himself look like the Messiah? Old Testament prophecies foretold: How he would die; How the people would react to his death;

That his side would be pierced; Where he would be buried; Where he would be born; When he would be born; The virgin birth; and His betrayal. These are eight different prophecies, and it is impossible for Jesus to have purposely fulfilled them. While hanging on the cross, how would he have purposely fulfilled having the spear stuck in his side? How would he have fulfilled the prophecy of the guards casting lots for his clothes? How would he have purposely fulfilled being born of a virgin and in Bethlehem at a certain time in history? These things were out of his control. The chances of just one person fulfilling all eight of these prophecies is 1 out of 100,000,000,000,000,000, or 1 out of 10^{17}.[65]

I love the way Stoner (author of the previous quote) illustrated the meaning of this number. He asked the reader to imagine filling the State of Texas knee deep in silver dollars. Include in this huge number one silver dollar with a black check

---

[65] http://www.rtgmin.org/2012/06/08/prophecies-jesus-fulfill/

mark on it. Then, turn a blindfolded person loose in this sea of silver dollars. The odds that the first coin he would pick up would be the one with the black check mark are the same as eight prophecies being fulfilled accidentally in the life of Jesus.

The point, of course, is that when people say that the fulfillment of prophecy in the life of Jesus was accidental, they do not know what they are talking about. Keep in mind that Jesus did not just fulfill eight prophecies, He fulfilled 108. The chances of fulfilling sixteen is 1 in 10^{45}. When you get to a total of 48, the odds increase to 1 in 10^{157}. Accidental fulfillment of these prophecies is simply beyond the realm of possibility.[66]

Can you imagine? For only eight of these prophesies being fulfilled, it is like pulling out a specific silver dollar from an area the size of the whole state of Texas, knee deep in silver dollars. The odds of this are 1 in 100,000,000,000,000,000. It would be nearly impossible to pick the right coin by chance.

Therefore the odds of Jesus fulfilling these prophesies by mere chance are inconceivable.

---

[66] http://lamblion.com/articles/articles_bible6.php

The Deaths of Great Men

The deaths of these religious leaders can help you decide which to follow.

It is commonly believed that Buddha died of food poisoning at eighty years of age, in 483 BC. Some say his cause of death was the eating of poisonous, wild mushrooms.

An enslaved Jewish woman reportedly poisoned Mohammad. He had taken her captive after destroying her community and relatives, and she killed him for it. It is said by some that his death was slow.

Bahá'u'lláh was reportedly poisoned by his brother, over a rivalry for power. He was believed to die from the results of this poisoning, many years later.

A mob killed Joseph Smith while he was being held in jail on charges of treason by the State of Illinois.

Charles Taze Russel died of urinary bladder inflammation.

Moses died at 120 years old, and was buried by God.

Abraham died of old age, at 175 years.

Jesus died on a cross at the hands of Rome. He then rose from the dead three days later, never to die again. Forty days later, he ascended to Heaven in the view of His followers.

Conclude from this what you will. It seems obvious to me that Jesus's death marks him as unique. The others were killed or died under relatively mundane circumstances. And they stayed dead. Jesus rose from the grave in view of many and dwelt with them for many days afterward before ascending to Heaven. If nothing else, the extraordinary circumstances of his death and resurrection are powerful indicators that Jesus was more than an ordinary man.

What Did They Say?

In order to decide whom to follow, it is important to understand whom these religious leaders thought they were. Remember each thought he was chosen by God to deliver a message. Each had a different experience.
You can tell a lot about these teachers through this.

One could say for example, the boss told me to tell you to get to work. This is significant, wouldn't you say? But what if one comes saying he is the Boss?

1) Bahá'u'lláh was a messenger from God.
2) Mohammad was a messenger from God.
3) Charles Taze Smith was a Christian reformer.
4) Joseph Smith was a restorer of the Church of Jesus Christ.
5) Buddha was a man enlightened to the truth and a teacher of this way of living.
6) Abraham was the first Jew and father of the Jewish religion. Christians and Muslims point to him as the father of their religions.

7) Moses was a prophet who received the Ten Commandments of God. He also acted as the judge over the Jewish people.
8) Jesus was the Son of God, the equal to God. He said there was no way to God except through him. He performed many miracles and was understood to be God incarnate by His followers.

Each one recognized his mortality, and the fact that he was merely a man. Each stated that he was chosen to deliver a message as a servant of God.

There are two exceptions: Buddha and Jesus.

Buddha did not believe in the existence of God. He was only giving the truth as he had become aware of it through personal revelation.

Jesus, on the other hand, claimed divinity. He is the only world religious leader who has. He proclaimed exclusivity and devotion to himself and his message.

There is a significant difference between Jesus and the others. They all recognize themselves as enlightened messengers, and some believed they were reformers.

Jesus stands in a different category, all by himself. He claims to be God, not a messenger, not an enlightened man, and not a mere reformer. According to him:

> I am the way and the truth and the life. No one comes to the Father except through me. If you really knew me, you would know my Father as well. From now on, you do know him and have seen him.[67]

---

[67] *John 14:6–7*

Why Some Do Not Trust

Now that we have laid out all the facts, you might be thinking, "Why *wouldn't* a person choose Jesus?" Over many years of discussions with people, I have come to believe that all reasons for not choosing him are just excuses. Some might give reasons like, "How could Noah put all those animals on the ark?" or "Miracles can't happen, so Jesus performed no miracles." I've heard people say that Jesus's message is not truly understood, because "The Bible has been changed!" or "The Catholics changed Christianity!"

There are answers to all these excuses, based on evidence and logic, but skeptics refuse to consider the lack of logic in their own reasoning. Their true problem with the Bible is simply that they want to do what they want to do! The implications of following Jesus's guidance are just too restrictive for many.

But I ask, "Why are we so resistant to the love he exemplified?" Everyone recognizes his inherent goodness. Everyone says the world would be great if everyone would love. We are all asking for social justice, equality, and peace, so why are we resisting the one person who exemplified all of this? (I think I know the answer: We want others to be loving people while reserving the right to be an ass!)

Sir Julian Huxley highlights how people seek answers that fulfill their personal desires rather than those that are true. When asked why evolution had become so popular, he said, "I suppose the reason we all jumped at 'Origin of Species' was because God interfered with our sexual morals."[68] That is, that we preferred to believe in evolution rather than creation because we liked that answer better, not because it was any more true. Let's be honest—we rarely base our concept of what is true on the facts, but rather base it on our preference.

Unfortunately, this is the most deadly approach to living life. Worse, it could leave us irretrievably damned.

I understand why we approach life this way. We are afraid of change, we like it how it is, and we do not want to rock the boat. I have encountered multiple men who have confessed a desire to follow Christ, yet have given dubious

---

[68] http://sensuouscurmudgeon.wordpress.com/2009/11/12/creationist-wisdom-%E2%80%94-example-81/

reasons for why they do not. They are worried about what they might lose. Their wife might not like the change. They have friends and hobbies that would be affected. It is just easier to put their fingers in their ears and sing "lalala!" in order to drown out the truth.

There is a tension between how much I want life to be a certain way and how likely I think that what Jesus said was true. We may think, "Well, Jesus may be right and the most reasonable person to trust, but I like my life and I won't risk it because Jesus may be wrong." But if what Jesus says is true, then we must change. I believe that the more a person fights the guidance of Jesus, the more desperate he is for the facts to disappear.

We must decide in spite of desire, of fear, and of the risk of impending change. Decisive action is required as protection against the possibility of punishment.

And this takes courage, I will not deny that.

We all have the free will to decide. As Jimi Hendrix said, "I'm the one that's got to die when it's time for me to die, so let me live my life the way I want to." But before you decide not to decide, remember that the way you live affects how you die, and that something happens afterward! Hunkering down in denial only puts off the inevitable; the dark cloud is coming and no meteorologist can stop it!

Conclusion

From multiple perspectives, we have found Jesus to be the most viable candidate to trust as our guide to the afterlife. He is the most reasonable to trust. After all, he is the most commonly exalted and admired of all religious leaders.

We all die and something happens after the fact. This is a serious matter for all of us and our loved ones. This is a fact that no one can deny.

We don't know what happens after we die. This is also irrefutable. We have preferences and opinions, but as we have all learned through life, a thing is not so merely because we want it to be. We have never experienced the glories or horrors of the afterlife. The only man who has, and come back to tell the tale, is Jesus himself.

We are all in the same box. Because we cannot know for certain who is right, we must decide whom we can trust. I hope you have concluded with me that we cannot entrust our souls to emotionally driven opinions. We need a critical, sensible way to determine what way to follow.

We are not dealing in absolutes, but rather in probabilities. We are all accustomed to this—we make decisions based on probability every day. We vote, marry, take jobs, move, and choose careers not based on guaranteed positive outcomes, but on the probability of positive outcomes. With the information we have, we make judgments.

The other day, I made a poor decision. I kicked a guy out of my house whom I was helping to quit a drug addiction. With the information I knew of him and the situation we found ourselves in, it seemed obvious that he had stolen money from my son's room. With the information I had, I was led to a conclusion based on probabilities. This was the final straw after many other infractions, and so I sent him away.

But I was wrong!

About a week later, I found that my son's friend had come to the house and picked up the money, which was actually his, without telling anyone.

I lacked a bit of information in my analysis of the situation, and failed to make the correct decision.

Thus, what seems obvious is not always true. We must make sure to gather all the information that is available in order to make the right choice. We must not dismiss information because it doesn't suit our preferences.

I have heard people say, "My parents made me go to church when I was a kid, so I hate religion," "My pastor ran off with the church secretary, so they are all hypocrites!" and "Catholic priests molest children, so I want no part of religion." This is just a sampling of reasons people give to opt out of religion. However, no one says, "I hate education because my parents made me go to school six hours a day for twelve years" or "I no longer watch boxing because Mike Tyson bit Evander Holyfield's ear!"

This is because everyone recognizes that these are ludicrous arguments. The state of your soul should not be determined by your emotions, preferences, and imagination, but rather through hard reasoning.

We die, something happens, and we do not know what it is. Some say that they know what happens. We are left to decide whom to entrust with our soul.

I have heard people say, "I think God is good and I do not think a good God would put anyone in Hell. I'm a good person, and God wouldn't put me in Hell."

I once thought this way, as well. That is what I preferred to believe. It gave me room to live as I chose, unhindered by religion. Not that I knew much or thought much about religion growing up—I suspect this is because I am not from a religious family. My parents were good, hard-working Americans, and we did not attend church. As I have mentioned earlier in this book, my idea of the afterlife was simple but misguided: "If there is a God, I'm sure He put me here to have a good time. And I won't disappoint Him!"

The truth is we do not know much for certain. We are stuck either foolishly trusting ourselves (and what do we know about the afterlife?) or have faith in someone who has more insight. Certainly, we should not blindly follow the first idiot who says he knows, but instead look critically at the options.

Some wonder, "Why doesn't God just show Himself and solve the mystery and fix all the problems?" I do not know the answer, although I have suspicions due to my trust in Jesus and what I have learned from the Bible. Nevertheless, wouldn't you say it is a little presumptuous for you to decide the parameters of the universe and then demand that God submit to these? He would hardly be God, if that were the case. Have a little perspective. In the movie The Avengers, Nick Fury tries to avert war by saying, "We have no quarrel with your people." To which the antagonist answers, "An ant has no quarrel with a boot."[69]

That is, it does no good to argue your point of view when it comes to God. He is the Creator, He has all the knowledge and power, and so His is the point of view that matters!

In some way, all religions point to Jesus. He is admired by them all as a miracle worker, a man sent by God, a prophet, an example from God, a savior, the son of God, and God in the flesh. He is admitted to be an exemplary man by all major religions—by those who preceded him as well as those who followed.

Jesus is the most credible. It was prophesied that he would come and die on a cross and rise from the dead. He

---

[69] *The Avengers.*

did this before the people of Jerusalem, before his enemies and friends, before Jews and Romans. He ate and visited with over five hundred witnesses in the forty days after he rose, and then they watched him ascend into the sky with a promise to return. The Jews, Muslims, Bahá'ís, Mormons, Jehovah's Witnesses, and Christians all attest to him coming again.

All of the other religions are legitimized by accounts of unverifiable events from these great leaders. Mohamed said that he saw an angel in private, Joseph Smith said that he saw an angel in private, and Bahá'u'lláh said that he saw an angel in private. Siddhartha Gautama's ideas are legitimized only in that they come from himself, and we can believe he did not lie about his belief. Hinduism was generated from various tribal beliefs over thousands of years. The Jews rejected Jesus and are still waiting for the Messiah's coming, in spite of the prophesies Jesus fulfilled.

Each religion has a form of punishment for evil doers. In some, you cease to exist, others have a short-term punishment with terms of release, and Islam and Christianity both teach that damnation is eternal. Using a worst-case analysis, Islam and Christianity are the best ways to avoid the worst punishment. Because Islam is self-refuting, the safe choice is Jesus.

Through three different modes of analysis, we find that Jesus is the only choice. He is the one world religious leader that we need to appeal to. All roads lead to him!

The Message

So say that you trust Jesus. After you have considered all the perspectives and conducted a thorough analysis, you decide to trust his guidance. According to him, eternal life is a context that we are born into. It is the reality we live in. The next question to ask Jesus is, "How do I get Heaven and avoid Hell?"

According to the New Testament, a wealthy young guy once met Jesus and asked him the question we all would ask him if we met him face-to-face. "How do I go to Heaven?" he asked.

Jesus responded to him, "You know the commandments: 'Do not murder, do not commit adultery, do not steal, do not give false testimony, do not defraud, honor your father and mother.'"[70]

The young man responded that he had done this since he was a kid. Then Jesus says, "Go, sell everything you have and give to the poor, and you will have treasure in heaven. Then come, follow me."[71]

---

[70] Mark 10:19, New International Version of the Bible
[71] Mark 10:21, New International Version of the Bible

The young man left despondent, feeling that Jesus was asking too much. Jesus then turned to His followers and said,

I tell you the truth . . . no one who has left home or brothers or sisters or mother or father or children or fields for me and the gospel will fail to receive a hundred times as much in this present age (homes, brothers, sisters, mothers, children and fields—and with them, persecutions) and in the age to come, eternal life.[72]

On another occasion, a priest asked Jesus the same question:

"Teacher," he asked, "what must I do to inherit eternal life?"
"What is written in the Law?" [Jesus] replied. "How do you read it?"
He answered: "Love the Lord your God with all your heart and with all your soul and with all

---

[72] Mark 10:29, New International Version of the Bible

your strength and with all your mind; and Love your neighbor as yourself."

"You have answered correctly," Jesus replied. "Do this and you will live."

But [the priest] wanted to justify himself, so he asked Jesus, "And who is my neighbor?"

In reply, Jesus said: "A man was going down from Jerusalem to Jericho, when he fell into the hands of robbers. They stripped him of his clothes, beat him and went away, leaving him half dead. A priest happened to be going down the same road, and when he saw the man, he passed by on the other side. So too, a Levite, when he came to the place and saw him, passed by on the other side. But a Samaritan, as he traveled, came where the man was; and when he saw him, he took pity on him. He went to him and bandaged his wounds, pouring on oil and wine. Then he put the man on his own donkey, took him to an inn and took care of him. The next day he took out two silver coins and gave them to the innkeeper. 'Look after him,' he said, 'and when I return, I will reimburse you for any extra expense you may have.'

"Which of these three do you think was a neighbor to the man who fell into the hands of robbers?"

The expert in the law replied, "The one who had mercy on him."

Jesus told him, "Go and do likewise."[73]

Go do likewise! You can see that Jesus requires love and compassion to be the center of our understanding and practice. When we ask Jesus how to have eternal life, his answer is to love God and love your neighbor. Jesus further clarifies by emphasizing the importance of helping those in need.

It is not God's plan for us to walk by a person in need. Such behavior is not consistent with those going to Heaven. The Samaritan who helped the man in need is an example of the love that God requires. This is how to get eternal life—we must trust Jesus and, as a result, follow his instruction. To the question of how to go to Heaven,

---

[73] Luke 10:25–37, New International Version of the Bible

Jesus's answer was the same: Live your life to serve the one in need!

This is believing, this is devotion, this is revelation, and this is worship: following Jesus means to be like Jesus.

Now, some of you may be confused at this point. You have heard through friends, family, Christian pastors, radio, T.V., and books that all you need to do is believe in Jesus in order to be saved.

We have been inundated with this oversimplified message. It has been reiterated so much that it has become the mantra of how to go to heaven and avoid the punishment of Hell.

And this mantra has been an obstacle for many. A person who does not follow Jesus hears this and thinks that it is ridiculous to think that belief can equal salvation. I agree! The fact is that Jesus emphasizes that it takes an entirely different approach to find salvation.

Jesus asserts that if you believe him, then you will do what he says. Yes, belief is a part of the equation, but it is only the start. The proof of your belief is your heeding of his words.

Sure, the wealthy young guy believed that Jesus was special, but he did not believe in Jesus so much that he was willing to follow Jesus's advice. It is reasonable that the young man responded as he did. How did Jesus know for sure? Did he truly have the inside track on this? If Jesus had asked less, perhaps the young man would have believed. But then, if salvation was so easy, then it would not be necessary to believe.

This is the key difference between saying you believe and getting the reward for believing: the reward is yours only if your actions echo your belief.

Your Choice

What must you do? Since death is unavoidable, it is important to do what you can to ensure that your afterlife is not a torment. There are three options: do nothing, decide your own path, or follow Jesus. You should make your decision the centerpiece of your life. After all, you cannot wish death away.

To do nothing is a frightening risk. I know we cannot know for sure about God and the afterlife, but to do nothing is to give up on the hope of your salvation. And how will it feel on your death bed, as you lie there wondering what is next, wondering whether or not it will be pleasant when you wake up on the other side? Will your Creator be there to embrace you, will you receive a brutal blow to welcome you to a new life of excruciation, or will you fade to a blissful nothingness?

We have come to the conclusion that Jesus is the most rational choice. Each and every one of the world's major religions point to him, he is the most credible, and to follow him helps you to avoid the most extreme punishment among all.

My personal experience with Jesus has not been that he took away the life I thought I wanted. Rather, he has given me a new and better life. I had a great career as a nuclear engineer and a loving, supportive family, but I did not have answers for the big question. It has been very challenging to live this new lifestyle of love, nonetheless I will never go back!

Now, my great dream is that the whole world will live in real sacrificial love! The world is waiting for you.

We imagine that the cost of following Jesus is much more difficult than it actually is. In fact, it is not hard to love. I have suffered in many ways by following Jesus, but I could never turn back to my old life as nice as it was. I do not regret this choice in spite of the difficulties. The benefits are inherent in the call to love. You can't truly know it until you are in it—it is a gift from God to the faithful.

We grow to love. From experience to experience we get better at seeing who needs our help and responding selflessly.

We cannot know for sure what happens after death, but we can try to find the best outcomes for our afterlives if we choose the right path. As this book shows, Jesus is our best option. There are many other works that show why we can trust the Bible and Jesus. Books like *Evidence that Demands a Verdict* and *More Than a Carpenter* by Josh McDowell are very informative, and C.S. Lewis's book *Mere Christianity* is great, also. Lee Strobel also has a few books on the subject, which are available at http://www.leestrobel.com.

I hope that this book is only your starting point on the quest to discover the truth.

> "Jesus answered, 'I am the way
> and the truth and the life.
> No one comes to the Father
> except through me.'"[74]

---

[74] John 14:6, New Testament, New International Version

Appendix: Argument Simplified

1. We all die
2. Something happens
3. No one knows for sure what happens
4. We have to trust someone in order to understand what happens.
5. We must consider whom we trust, and why.

The following is a chart to help see how each type of person will fare compared to each religion in the afterlife.

Comparison Chart

Religion	Good Person	Budd	Hind	Bahá'í	Morm	J.W.s	Jud	Islam	Christ
Good Person	H	H	H	H	H	Pn	Pt	Pe	Pe
Budd	H	H	H	H	H	Pn	Pt	Pe	Pe
Hind	H	H	H	H	H	Pn	Pt	Pe	Pe
Bahá'í	H	H	H	H	H	Pn	Pt	Pe	Pe
Morm	H	H	H	H	H	Pn	Pt	Pe	Pe
J.W.s	H	H	H	H	H	H	Pt	Pe	Pe
Jud	H	H	H	H	H	Pn	H	Pe	Pe
Islam	H	H	H	H	H	Pn	Pt	H	Pe
Christ	H	H	H	H	H	Pn	Pt	Pe	H

H = Heaven Pn = Annihilation Pt = Temporary Punishment Pe = Eternal Punishment

Note: Assumes that you adhere to the particular religious practices of the religion you identify with.

In the Buddhist, Hindu, Baha'i, and Mormon religions, there is no punishment for those who are just being good. If any of these religions are true, then practitioners all end up in the same place as the "good people," although in Mormonism the practitioners go to a high heaven, whereas the "good people" are at a lower level of heaven.

If the Jehovah's Witnesses are right, those of us who are not Jehovah's Witnesses will cease to exist after death.

Both Islam and Christianity carry the greatest condemnation for sin: eternal punishment in Hell. Islam is

self-refuting, however, which leaves Jesus as the best possible option for avoiding the worst punishment.

Thus, of the two safest choices in the worst case analysis, Jesus is the most credible: his claims are verifiable by witnesses, who became martyrs to proclaim his resurrection.

All the major world religions acknowledge and revere Jesus. Of all the other religious leaders, Jesus is the only one to claim to be God, as no other dared. Furthermore, he satisfied the Messianic prophesies of the Old Testament written hundreds of years before his birth, which identified him as the Savior.

Choose Your Superhero

Analysis	Hind.	Bud.	Mohammad	Bahá'u'lláh	Smith	Russell	Jesus
Origin							X
Worst Case							X
Testament							X
Odds							X
Deaths							X
Identity							X

X-Most probable world religious leader to be trusted.

The first suggested reading in the Bible is the book of John in the New Testament and Matthew, chapters 5–7 and 25.

Good luck in your pursuit, and may God's mercy be upon you.

About the Author

Cliff Williams is a pastor and missionary. He lives with his wife and six children north of Seattle, Washington.

Cliff studied engineering at Washington State University and worked as a nuclear engineer. After completing service in the Air Force National Guard, he and his family served street kids in Colombia, South America. With the help of a team of friends, Cliff has planted two churches in the U.S. Northwest.

Cliff is currently working with others to help the poor of the community to undergo drug/alcohol rehabilitation, to find housing, and to develop their careers. He is also working on economic development in poor countries. All income generated by the sales of these books goes to this work.

More Books by Clifford E. Williams

You can purchase this book and other titles by Clifford E. Williams as ebooks or paperback from Amazon.com.

Rules for Christian Radicals **points out how to overcome the ineffectiveness of Christian institutions. The book deals primarily with the model of sacrificial living not as a great idea from Christianity but as a mandate from Christ.**

Book of the Poor **is a clarion call for a resurgence of compassion, to reestablish the Church as the mission of hope, and to care with a renewed mercy for all who suffer.**

You can visit him on Facebook under Cliff Williams and visit his blog at operationdeluge.com. You can also listen to his radio broadcast on kgnw.com.

www.ingramcontent.com/pod-product-compliance
Lightning Source LLC
Chambersburg PA
CBHW060755050426
42449CB00008B/1409